How to Stop Whining and Start Winning

A Guide to Goal Setting and Time Management

Mark Riesenberg

KENDALL/HUNT PUBLISHING COMPANY
4050 Westmark Drive   Dubuque, Iowa 52002

Copyright © 1996, 1997, 1999 by Human Resources Unlimited

ISBN 0-7872-6417-2

All rights reserved. No part of this publication may be reproduced, stored in a retrieval system, or transmitted, in any form or by any means, electronic, mechanical, photocopying, recording, or otherwise, without the prior written permission of the copyright owner.

Printed in the United States of America

10   9   8   7   6   5   4   3   2   1

The Results People Are Getting

"This book is incredible! It doesn't quit, page after page is filled with practical ideas. It's a winner."

James L. Evers
Author of **How to Tap Your Peak Performance for Any Task**

"The power of setting goals is real. When Mark was coaching me, I told him I wanted to be promoted on my birthday. Three months later I was, and I love my new job! Now I believe that I can achieve anything, once I have a clear vision of what it is that I want."

Dorothy Szlagor
Sales Manager, SRDS

"Beau . . . tiful. We have a system for success in our industry. Mark Riesenberg showed us how to implement and truly succeed with this system. You gave us the words on how to set goals, and how to run a team goal achievement meeting. The atmosphere in our office for the past year is electric, because we're making money!"

Joseph D. DiMento, CLU, ChFC
General Agent, John Hancock Financial Services

"Goal setting makes the decision making process, prioritizing, getting things in balance easier. It gives you a competitive advantage since most people don't set goals, and goal setting keeps my focus on the client. Our commitment to goal setting, and Mark Riesenberg, have helped us with all of the above."

William T. Bisson, Jr.
Publisher, **Pensions and Investments**

"Helped me personally and our sales people to focus on positive activities that kept us moving forward in a purposeful manner."

Dick Ryan
Advertising Director, **Investment News**

"Here is a practical action-oriented guide to time management. It will add value to your career . . . to your life."

Betty Jean Flagg
President, Flagg Brothers, Inc.

"As an investment consultant for almost 30 years, I have seen when employees have their financial lives in order, they're happier, more productive employees. This book will help you set goals that can move you towards greater financial freedom."

Richard Rodman, CFS, CPC
President, Tax Relief Investments, Inc.

"Mark's ideas for goal setting are electric. They become light for bringing life into a clearer direction. His energy and innovativeness are a delight."

Ardath Rodale
Chairman, Rodale Press, Inc.

"The concepts make sense, and are easy to apply. They allow the reader to stay focused, while entertained, resulting in increased revenue, clearer goals, and most importantly, a balanced life."

Joy J. D. Baldridge, CPC
President, Baldridge Seminars International

"Bottom line. Goal setting gives you so much more direction in the short and in the long term. You are more focused during the day which makes for a more powerful day, week, month, year, and life. It helps our representatives to be better self-starters. Their personal goals motivate them to be more successful in their territories."

Gary Grewal
Director of Sales Training,
Organon Pharmaceuticals

"We all talk about setting goals. Mark Riesenberg shows people how to get past the talking and on to the doing. Mark demonstrates the why, the how, and the benefit of goal setting with techniques that can be applied every day of our lives. The result is a better focus toward accomplishment of specific goals, both personal and professional."

Dennis Merlo
Executive Director, Training & Development,
The Purdue Frederick Company

Contents

Acknowledgments   ix
Preface   xi

Part I • *The Challenge of Success* _____ 1

1 WHY ARE SOME PEOPLE
MORE SUCCESSFUL THAN OTHERS?   3
   What Is Success?   3
   Back to the Basics, the Fundamentals   4
   The Four Aces of Success   5

2 WHAT HOLDS PEOPLE BACK?   7
   Whining   9
   Myths & Excuses   11

3 WHAT PROPELS PEOPLE FORWARD?   13
   Success: The Challenge of Balance   14
   Absorption   17
   Goals   18
   The Glue   18

Part II • *The Power of Goals* _____ 21

4 THE GOAL ACHIEVEMENT PROCESS (G.A.P.)   23
   Experience the Power of Planning   25
   Guaranteed Results   29
   The Two Pains   29

5 STEPS IN THE GOAL ACHIEVEMENT PROCESS   31
   The 5 W's and the 1 H—What We Will Be Covering   31
   Focus   31
   The Classic Study on Goals   33
   Don't Think It, Ink It   36
   Why Don't People Set Goals?   37

vi Contents

6 A SYSTEM: WHAT IT TAKES TO EXCEED YOUR GOALS—A FIVE STEP PROCESS 45
   It All Starts with Desire 45
   Step II: Belief 46
   Step III: Write It Down 47
   Getting Ready to Write 56
   Values 56
   Primed 60
   Oxymoron 61
   Prime Time 66
   An Inventory of Your Goals, Your Dreams 67
   Step IV: How To . . . Part Deux . . . The Three P's 70
   The When and Where of Goal Setting 72
   Where? 75
   The One-Part 75
   The Four-Part 77
   The Tri-Fold 77
   The Possibilities/Dream Form 79
   Carry, Look, and Work 81
   Save Your Goals As a Journal 84
   Visualization 84

7 IT STARTS AND ENDS WITH DESIRE 87
   Step V: Determination and Persistence 87
   The Goal Achievement Curve 89
   Everything Is a Process 91
   The Path of Mastery 92
   Some Additional Tips 93
   Reasons 93
   Inspect What You Expect 94
   Two Quotes 95
   Back to a K.I.S.S. 96

Part III • *Time Management* 97

8 NOW, YOU NEED TIME MANAGEMENT 99
   86,400: Your Greatest Asset 99
   Going the Distance 101
   Carpe Diem 101
   The Greatest Story Ever Told . . .
      About Time Management 102
   I'm Against Using "To Do" Lists 105
   The 80/20 Rule: Coming Back to a K.I.S.S. 106

No Whining, No Trying, No Guilt . . . Everybody Is a
      Procrastinator   107
   So, There Are Just Two Things to Know, and Do   108

**9 MINIMIZING AND ELIMINATING TIME WASTERS,
   PLUS HOW TO HANDLE THOSE INTERRUPTIONS   111**
   Be Ruthless with Time, But Gracious with People. Now,
      On to Handling Interruptions   111
   Time Wasters   112
   Knowing for Sure . . . Log It   114
   Time Management Techniques,
      Saving Two Hours a Day   114
   Strategies and Techniques for Handling Interruptions,
      and for Eliminating Time Wasters   116
   Problem: Personal Disorganization,
      Lack of Self-Discipline   117
   Clutter's Last Stand   117
   The Four D's   120
   The S.W.A.T. Team   121
   Problem: Procrastination   123
   Problem: Crisis Management/Fire Fighting   125
   Problem: Telephone/Voice Mail/E-Mail
      Interruptions   128
   Problem: Drop-In Visitors   130
   Problem: Attempting Too Much   131
   More Techniques With a Little Advice Mixed In   133
   The Most Common Techniques to Get and Stay
      Organized . . . The Five Major Parts   135
   Ah, That Clutter Thing Again   135
   A Step-by-Step Procedure to Get Uncluttered   136
   Knowledge is Potential Power, The Time
      Management Contract   139

**10 LOOKING FOR A FEW GOOD MANAGERS
   THE BIG SQUEEZE   141**
   Add, Delete, Fine-Tune   142
   Peer Group Review Associations   142
   Managing Multiple Priorities—Doing More
      With Less   143

Part IV • *The Next Step*   **145**

11 THE MYSTICAL SIDE OF GOAL SETTING   147
    The Next Step   154
    Dharma   154
    My Mission and My Dharma   155
    A Heat Seeking Missile   156
    It's a Wrap—A Few Last Thoughts   157

12 WITH A LITTLE HELP FROM MY FRIENDS—
RESOURCES TO HELP YOU ON YOUR WAY   159
    Recommended Audiocassettes   159
    Recommended Books   160
    Motivational Quotes   163

Acknowledgments

Thank you to my wonderful wife Terry, for without her, as we both agree, I'd be meditating today somewhere in the Himalayas.

Thank you to my beautiful daughters Kate and Courtney, to my brother Rick, to my nephew Matthew, to my in-laws (Lucy, Joe, Lisa, and Meryl, who is also my fabulous editor), to my great family of aunts, uncles, cousins, and to my best friends forever, Alan, Nina and Joy. They have all made it a little bit easier for me to leave my beloved Himalayas . . . but that's a whole other book.

And, of course, thank you to my awesome parents. To my marvelous mother Shirley, who was my spiritual role model because of her great love and respect for people of all backgrounds. She died as she lived with great inner and outer beauty. To my father Max, the bravest and most honest person I have ever met. He died as he lived, courageously and unselfishly.

Preface

I was pregnant with this book for several years. I got this image of being pregnant from a book by Henry Miller. Henry described how he would get on a bus and people would offer him a seat. He was so filled with his book that it was obvious to people that he was with child. This image stayed with me for many years and accurately tells you how I felt about carrying this book within me.

So why listen to me and take the time to read this book? In fact, why another book on this topic? A classic statement of our culture is, "I don't have time to read a book on time management." Or as a CEO told me after a series of workshops at his company, "I heard a lot of great things about your seminars. Sorry I couldn't attend, I didn't have the time."

In 1932, the founder of IBM, Tom Watson, held the first Sales & Marketing Executives Club meeting. An article called "The Biggest Problem Facing American Business Today: Time Management" appeared in the first newsletter. Not much has changed.

So why another book? Because this one is easy to understand and to implement. Because this book will get you results, guaranteed. Here's some background to help you know who I am and why I believe I'm in a position to be of great help to you in the pursuit and achievement of your personal and professional goals.

In May of 1987 I started my own business, HUMAN RESOURCES UNLIMITED. My specialties are giving keynote addresses, giving workshops on the challenges of success and workshops on the fundamentals of effective selling. Since starting my business I have met and talked with thousands of sales and non-sales professionals. Quite often my seminar participants tell me that of all the topics I covered, they enjoyed and got the most out of the sessions on goal setting and time management.

When I got to the part of the workshop on goal setting and time management I would noticeably change. My body language became more powerful, and my confidence would soar. I really leaned into the material at this point, because I **knew** my audience would get a lot out of this section. I had no doubts, and was totally confident. So I started to change my business. I focused more workshops on goal setting, being assured that my clients would be getting me at my best. I was to become known to my clients as "The Goal Guy," "The Goal Meister," a kind of Johnny Appleseed of goals, spreading the good news about the power of goal setting, giving the gift of goals.

All trainers mention the importance of goal setting and time management. At best it's just touched upon; at worst, quickly glossed over. I decided to devote my full attention to these subjects. I found that for many of my clients, having poor goal setting and poor time management habits is an Achilles heel. This means that they have so many excellent skills going for them, but because of their poor organizational skills, they are sabotaged from reaching their full personal and professional potential. My calling is to help people in the areas of goal setting and time management. To help these skills complement and support their other skills. The results were there for the participants. What great congruency, me being at my best, talking about what I loved the most, and people getting results. So my expertise is in the field of organizational skills—goal setting and time management. This is how I can best be of service to you. How I can most effectively help you to positively change your life. I believe that using what you will learn in this book will get you the short, intermediate, and long-term results you desire. I can help you close the gap between desired and actual results. Thank you for this opportunity to be of service.

Oh, P.S. I walk the talk. I **do** what I talk and write about. My editor told me she had worked with about 100 authors. I asked her how many of them got their final manuscript in on time. Her answer: "Two!" I immediately promised her that I would be her third. I was. After all, I didn't want a book on time management not to be in on time.

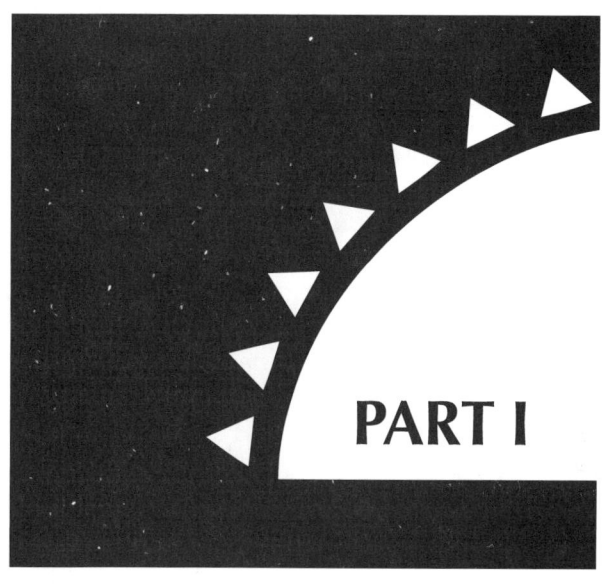

PART I

The Challenge of Success

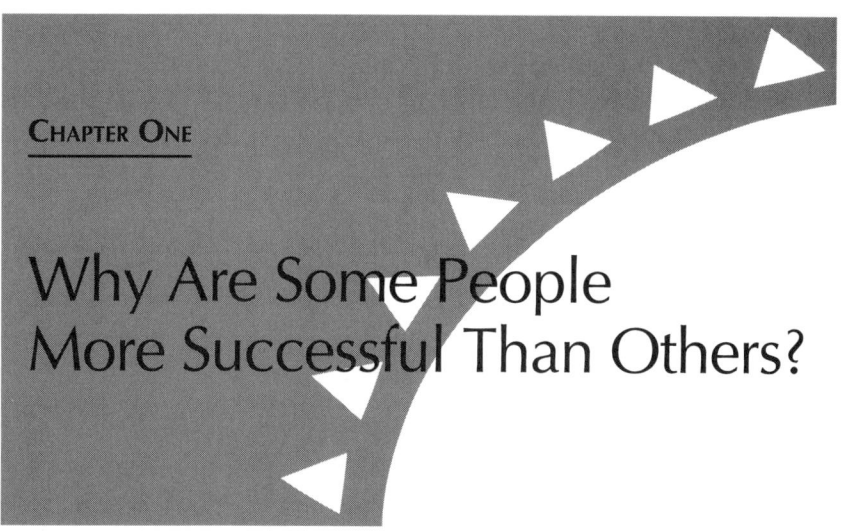

CHAPTER ONE

Why Are Some People More Successful Than Others?

What Is Success?

Goal setting can change your life . . . it can help you become more and more successful.

But, **what is success**?

When you think of success what comes to your mind? What pictures, images, words come to your mind to best describe success? What does it mean to you?

If you are like most of my audiences, what comes to mind might be some of the following: Happiness, Contentment, Power, Fame, Fortune, Working Your Way Up the Corporate Ladder, Running Your Own Business, Having A Loving and Supportive Family. There is no end to this list since each person has their own definition of what it means to be successful. Yes, I believe that there are over 5 billion different definitions for what success is. The classic definition of success, popularized by Earl Nightingale, is **the progressive realization of a worthy goal.** Here's my definition of success: **The intelligent, meaning conscious progress towards the use of your full potential**, *and* the inevitable realization of your full potential. We will explore each of these definitions in greater detail throughout this book.

So, **what is the greatest secret to success?** Another list: Hard Work, Perseverance, Honesty, Motivation, Drive, Skill, Intelligence, a Rich Parent, Luck. Again, this list could go on and on without ever wanting for a lack of correct answers.

But, take another hard look at the question. What is the greatest secret of success? When you look at the above answers, none of these is a secret! And that to me is the greatest secret to success, **that there are no secrets**! Everything we need to know about success is contained somewhere—in a book, an audiocassette, a video, a software package, in someone else's mind. It's there. Everything we need to know to be more successful is there for the asking and for the finding.

Back to the Basics, the Fundamentals

My role is to remind you about things you already know, but may not be using, to help you to be more and more successful. I have found that people, for the most part, need to be reminded more than they need to learn something new. And when it comes to success, that's what people need . . . to be reminded. Many times in my workshops people will say to me that they really didn't hear anything new. I had just reminded them about things they had already known but were not using, and I had motivated them to finally put this valuable information into use. As one person told me after one year of applying these goal achievement principles: "I learned nothing new from your seminars or book, but its changed my life."

When I ask the question, **"Do you believe that knowledge is power?"** nearly 100% say, "Yes." Then, I'll ask, "If you don't use that knowledge is it still power?" Most will then say, "No." **Knowledge is *potential* power**. It's about getting back to the basics, the fundamentals of success. It's about using what you know.

Here's a legendary story about getting back to the basics. It was said that Vince Lombardi, the Hall of Fame football coach, would start off every football summer training camp, whether the team was coming off of a Super Bowl championship, or a losing season, with these words. He would get the entire team around him on opening day and say, "This is a football". I have also heard it said that one of the players then said, "Coach, you're going too fast".

Another back to the basics example is from Coach John Wooden, another sports Hall of Famer, but from the game of basketball. The first day of practice, he would have all of his players work on putting on their sneakers, and then lacing them up! Whew, what a great message/lesson about the critical importance of being brilliant on the basics, of being totally committed to the fundamentals of success.

The Four Aces of Success

Not only am I going to remind you of the fundamentals of success, but I will also give you a kiss, actually a K.I.S.S. This is an acronym, a word representing the first letter of several words. Now some of you may be thinking, "I know that one, it means **keep it simple stupid**". Well, you're partially correct. Traditionally this is very strong advice given to salespeople. But I'm going to modernize it a little and refer to it as, **keep it short and simple**. Most of the successful people that I know have an uncanny way of explaining things in a way that is short, simple, to the point and easy to understand.

My K.I.S.S. centers around the 4 Aces of Success, actually the 4 Aces of Belief, which bring about success. The 4 things that you must believe in to maximize and speed up your success are:

- Believe in yourself.
- Believe in your product, service.
- Believe in your company.
- Believe in your manager. Actually this is a two way street, your manager needs to believe in you as well.

Believe in yourself. A person who believes that no matter what he wants, if he wants it badly enough, and long enough, believes he can have it. A person who believes that whatever he focuses his attention on, if it's important enough to him, can make it happen.

Believe in your product/service. Have you ever tried to sell something that you didn't believe in? When I say sell, I don't mean just salespeople. I mean selling an idea, a concept, perhaps a new project within your company or family. If you don't believe in it you can sell it for a while, but eventually you'll burn out from your lack of conviction. Those that believe in their product/service are those who believe that what they're proposing makes a positive difference for the people involved.

Believe in your company, be it large, mid-size, small, or a sole proprietorship. Believing that whatever you are pursuing, your company will be there with the necessary resources and systems to support you.

Believe in your manager, and **have a manager who believes in you**. Perhaps this is the most important belief of all. You can have all three beliefs in place, but if you don't have a manager who believes in you, all of your efforts can be sabotaged. Missing any one of the four will hold you back, but too often I have seen that just missing this one last factor can lead to unfulfilled plans and passions.

Having a manager that believes in you means having somebody that will give you the support, encouragement, praise that we all need from time to time. This kind of manager will give you the "tough love", positive feedback to help you self-correct, to help you stay on track when things aren't going quite your way.

CHAPTER TWO

What Holds People Back?

So now that we know that there is nothing new under the sun and that I'm here to remind you of the basics, the fundamentals of success, let's take a look at what holds people back.

I saw a list titled *The 14 Worst Human Fears*. A group of researchers simply approached 3,000 people and asked them to list their greatest fears. What do you think were some of the things on this list? If you said any of the following you were correct:

- Darkness
- Dogs
- Flying
- Death
- Sickness
- Financial Problems
- Insects/Bugs
- Heights
- Speaking Before A Group

These aren't all 14, but these are the ones that people guess correctly the most often. And what was #1? **The fear of public speaking!** Speaking before a group. By far and away. The researchers found that people mentioned this fear twice as much as any other fear, and way ahead of the fear of death, which simply means that many people would rather die than stand up and give a presentation in front of a group of people. I guess this means that he would rather be the person in the coffin rather than the person giving the eulogy. No wonder the industry of helping people with their presentation skills is a service in such great demand.

The #1 thing that holds people back is **fear**. Or, as I have sometimes seen it explained, F.E.A.R—False Evidence Appearing Real. The F.U.D. factor. If you get enough Fear, Uncertainty, and Doubt in your brains and veins, it will smash any dream, sometimes well before you have even gotten started putting your action plan into effect.

One fear that I believe is an umbrella fear, the root cause of many of our other fears, is tropophobia. Do you know what tropophobia is? Some guess the fear of the tropics. Several times I've heard people say the fear of orange juice. Good guesses, but not quite there. Tropophobia is the **fear of change**. We human beings hate change. We resist it and fight against it. It gives us a sense of being out of control, which obviously is a feeling many of us don't like.

Which brings us to the second thing that holds people back... **comfort zones**. We are creatures of habit. I have heard it said that 90% of what we do, day in and day out, is the same as the previous day. It has even been said that 90% of our thoughts are the same thoughts that we had the previous day. Why do we hate change so much? Try this simple little exercise, and I believe it will give you some great insight into why we hate change at such a gut level.

Sitting comfortably, fold your arms and look down to see which arm you crossed over the other. Now unfold your arms, and now fold them once again. If you're like most people you probably folded your arms the same way as you did the first time. Now fold your arms the other way. How does that feel? Probably a bit strange, awkward, weird, wrong ... uncomfortable. This is the power of habits.

Even when we intellectually know and emotionally feel that something is wrong for us, we still struggle to change. We know that a certain habit is bad for us, but we just keep on doing it over and over again. That's why people have such a difficult time changing. As Mark Twain said, quitting smoking isn't difficult. He's done it dozens of times. Even though we know it's not good for us, we get comfortable doing it just that way, and we aren't going to change.

It is not our habits that hold us back since many habits are positive addictions, actions that are positive for us. It is our bad habits that hold us back. Let me introduce you to what I believe is the worst habit in the world and the most contagious disease in the world. This one habit more than any other habit will hold you, your family, and your team back from realizing their full potential.

Whining

It is the habit of **WHINING**. By whining I mean the complaining, the criticizing, the blaming, the gossiping and the backstabbing that can go on and on, within your own mind, your family, or your company, no matter what the size of the firm.

Remember Doug and Wendy Whiner from Saturday Night Live? The Whiners. They would complain about anything and everything. "We have a reservation." "I have diverticulitis." "I hate when that happens." Actually, this last line is from another SNL character. "I'm too old, too young, too thin, too fat, over qualified, under qualified, too tall, too short." Just rolling from one problem to the next.

If you have children or are often in the company of children, you also know what I mean about whining. For children, whining can sometimes be positive. This is the beginning stages of developing excellent selling and negotiating skills. This is how the little people get the big people in their world to do what they want them to do. Tremendous persistence and never taking that first no seriously. But like most things of childhood, whining is something you need to leave behind as it develops into higher skills. My general rule of thumb is that whining is probably OK up to the age of 10. At least we can understand why a child whines.

Unfortunately I have met people in their teens, 20's, 30's, 60's, 80's, who are still whining. The whining that goes on in a person's mind such as, "I can't", "It's too hard", "It's impossible". A few more examples are, "I don't like it", "It's not fair", "I don't want to do it". The classic killer whine of a dying person, or a dying company, is this infamous whine, "But we've never done it that way before", or "We've always done it that way". See the **Killer Phrases** list (page 10) for more of these potential squashing, self-fulfilling prophecy statements.

A new idea is introduced, and around the water cooler are two or three people ripping this new idea, new program, apart. And before you know it, the negativity is spreading like wild fire throughout the company. Before the new idea is even implemented, it's dead in the water. That's why I call whining and negativity the most contagious diseases in the world. One or two people putting something down, and before you know it, it's spreading. Ever walk into a room where there are a lot of negative people? You can cut the thick feeling of tension and depression with a knife. With a whiner it's always going from one problem to the next. Let's take a look at the difference between a whiner and a winner.

There are always going to be problems, obstacles, and frustrations. It's just a reality check. So don't be surprised when they come

Killer Phrases
No Excuses, No Rational Lies

1. We've never done it that way before.

    or . . .

2. We've *always* done it that way.

3. Sounds good, but . . .*

    *but the great eraser of what was said before the but
    Note: It's your big **buts** that hold you back from success.
    i.e. I'll call on that account, but . . . ; I'll start exercising right away, but . . .

4. It's all right in theory, *but* can you put it into practice?

5. It won't work in our business.

6. Somebody would have done it if it was such a good idea.

7. It can't be such a good idea . . . since I was the one who thought of it.

    Note: How some people evaluate their own creativity, or lack of it.

8. It's not in the budget.

9. We don't have enough people.

10. You'll never be able to sell it to management.

11. We're too big a company for that.

12. There isn't enough time or money.

Truth: Keep on doing what you're doing . . . and you'll keep on getting what you got. Antidote: **Think outside the box** . . . and remember, *If it is to be it is up to me!*

Insanity is doing the same thing over and over again while expecting a different result.

up. A whiner and a winner react differently when the inevitable problems do come up. A whiner focuses 100% of his attention on the problem. He's really not all that concerned about solving the problem. All he does is go from one problem to the next.

But I'm not saying talking about problems makes you a whiner. What I am saying is that a whiner just puts all of his attention on the problem, where a winner focuses some of his attention on identifying the problem, discussing the problem. Here is where the difference comes in. The winner will then switch his attention off the problems and take the attitude, "OK, so what am I going to do about it?" Instead of being problem centered, he is solution oriented. Not an exact science, but kind of like the 80/20 rule which we will be discussing in detail when we get to time management. A winner puts approximately 20% of his attention on the problem and 80% on finding a solution. Instead of bringing everybody down with his negativity, as a whiner does, the problem discussion with a winner leads to the problem being solved.

Myths & Excuses

The third thing that holds people back is the myth about success. Myths are misunderstandings about what it takes to be successful in our society. For instance, the 5 greatest myths or misunderstandings about being successful in our society are (in no particular order of importance) the need to:

- have had good grades in school
- have an above average IQ
- have higher degrees of education
- come from a well connected family
- be good looking.

Oh well, for me 1 out of 5 isn't too bad. Thank goodness for that last one.

Now I'm not saying that these five things don't help, because obviously they do . . . but they don't assure success.

What happens with some people is that maybe they don't have one or two of these talents/skills/accomplishments in place. For instance, me. I was always in the third of the class that made the top two-thirds possible. Good grades and Mark Riesenberg just didn't go together. But what most people will do is use these "deficiencies", "shortcomings" as an **excuse** for why we can't be successful.

When we get to the second thing that propels people forward I will share with you research that totally shatters these myths about success and shows that anybody using these as a reason he can't be successful is merely making excuses.

"I never knew a person who was good at making excuses who was good at anything else." —Ben Franklin

CHAPTER THREE

What Propels People Forward?

Enough about what holds people back. Let's now put our attention on what propels people forward. We all have fears, do some whining, indulge ourselves in occasional negativity, and once in awhile make excuses for our lack of success. So let's now learn what we can do to minimize these weaknesses that are preventing us from using our full potential. We looked at three things that hold us back. Now we're going to look at three things that can propel us forward.

Write down the name of someone you consider successful. It can be an historical figure, someone who is no longer alive; it can be someone in today's limelight. It doesn't need to be someone famous. It can be a parent, a grandparent, a brother, a sister, another family member, a next door neighbor, a community member, your boss, someone you work with, or it can be yourself. Write down this person's name.

Now I'm going to give you 1-2 minutes. In this allotted time I want you to write down as many qualities and characteristics about this person you can think of, regarding what you believe propelled him to his success. Don't worry about giving the right answers. Just come up with as many words as you can think of that describe what you have found as qualities/characteristics of this successful person.

Your list will probably look a little like this:

Honest	Persistent
Intelligent	Hard Working
Creative	Risk Taker

Personable	Good Communicator
Motivated	Good Listener
Leader	Good Sense of Humor
Competent/Skillful	Good People Skills
Knowledgeable	Positive Mental Attitude
Integrity	Determined
Visionary	Courageous
Inspiring	Fair-Minded
Goal Oriented/Focused	Organized

Like our other lists, we could go on ad infinitum. But let's put our list aside for the moment.

Success: The Challenge of Balance

Time to talk about K.I.S.S. (Keep It Short & Simple) again. Everything that I have seen, read, or heard about success, from meeting people whom I consider successful, indicates that success simply comes down to two things. When you have these two things in place the world is truly your oyster.

The first thing is that every successful person whom I have ever met is skillful and really knows what they're talking about. Skillful, competent, talented individuals. They get tremendous respect from the people they work with because of this great knowledge they have about their chosen field of expertise.

But this isn't enough. Haven't you ever met people who seem to have everything going for them, people with great talent/skill but they're getting nowhere fast, or their careers seem to be spiraling downward? It's because skill by itself is not enough to bring about sustained success. Something else needs to be in **balance**.

This is a word that I'm very passionate about. In fact, my vanity plate (also called by its softer version, personal plate) on my car is **BALANCE**. I'm passionate about this because I have met too many "successful" people whom I don't consider successful at all. Oh yes, maybe they have accomplished a lot professionally. But when you look at their personal lives, nothing to be proud of, be it from different abuses such as drugs, alcohol, family violence or depression and unhappiness. Or, back to that person who has all this talent but seems to be getting nowhere fast. It's because skill alone cannot make him successful. What needs to be in balance is what some people have called the most important word in the English language . . .

ATTITUDE. By attitude I don't mean just positive thinking, even though I'd always rather opt to be a positive thinker over a negative one. I mean an individual who feels in his heart and in his mind that whatever he puts his attention to, he can make it happen. A "can do" attitude. A positive believer, a positive knower. Not only a competent person, but also a confident person. The balance of competence and confidence.

For me, when you have both of these, skill and attitude, in place, it is the foundation for great success, personally and professionally. And I say both because I have met people with wonderful attitudes, but they don't know what they're talking about. They haven't developed the necessary skills. These are people who have wonderful personal lives, but professionally have never accomplished as much or influenced their community as much as they might have.

Think of it this way:

*Knowledge is the **what to**, knowing where you need to be skillful.*
*Skill is the **how to**, mastering that particular discipline.*
*Attitude is the desire, the **want to**, putting into action what you know.*

When all three of these are working together, this is what builds integrity and character. This is where what you say you're going to do, and what you actually do, are congruent. Your habits, knowledge, goals, and plans support one another. You do what you say and choose to do. You know what to do, you know how to do it, and you do it. What we want is both personal and professional success, and that comes about through the balance of skill and attitude, which is the first thing that propels people forward.

Before we move on to the second point that propels people forward, let me share with you the qualities and characteristics I would expect to find in a successful person.

He would be able to do and experience the following:

- Balance a rich private life, with a fulfilling professional life.
- Be involved in a career that he was totally committed to and passionate about, regarding his positive influence on his family and his community.
- He would know how to balance rest with activity.

He would be an individual who knows how to turn it on (knowing how to summon up at will) through his positive physical habits, the energy necessary to be alive, awake, and alert. And he would know how to turn it off, knows how to relax, deeply relax, the kind of relaxation that prepares him once again for his demanding and fulfilling activity. I believe that this is the key to a balanced life, the very essence of what it means to be a balanced individual. A person that knows and experiences profound, deep rest, along with fulfilling dynamic activity. As you will find out in part two on goal setting, I believe that, professionally, the habit of setting goals is one of the most important things you can do for your success. But knowing how to rest and rejuvenate yourself at demand is the most important thing you can do personally. With this in mind here are the qualities I look for in a successful person and obviously, in myself.

- **Peace of Mind/Happiness:** I mean, "What's it all about, Alfie?" It's about this, the goal of all goals, why we do what we do. The pursuit and achievement of happiness. The natural tendency of life is to move towards more and more. One philosopher whom I respect said it simply, "The expansion of happiness is the purpose of life."
- **Physical Fitness/Health and Energy:** Eat right, exercise and get the proper amount of rest = ENERGY! Listen to your body, do your homework, your research to discover what each of these mean to you. It's different for everybody. As William Blake so profoundly put it: "Energy is bliss."
- **People Skills/Love:** What is success without love?
- **Financial Independence:** Simply the freedom from the worry about money. What income will free you up from constantly worrying about money? This amount is different for everybody.
- **Goals, Ideals, Values, Dreams, A Mission:** Knowing your purpose in life.
- **Focus on Strengths:** Successful people know their strengths and maximize on them, and also know how to minimize their weaknesses.
- **Life Long Learning:** A commitment to self-education beyond just the classroom and graduation from formal schooling.
- **Personal Fulfillment:** Being a person who indeed does have goals, but enjoys the moment, the present. Not being someone who is in the habit of thinking, "I'll be happy when". Happy when you get out of school, happy when you have your first job, happy when you have a certain level of income, happy when you get married, happy when you have children, happy when you get divorced. Successful people are happy *now*.

Absorption

Now, let's talk about the research that I had mentioned earlier, that will totally shatter the myths, the excuses about success and bring us to the second feature that propels people forward.

The researchers followed 1,500 people over a twenty year period. These were people with the same educational, socio-economic backgrounds. At the end of the twenty years, they found out that 63, a little less than 5%, had become self-made millionaires. When they interviewed these 63, they found that they shared many qualities, but that there was just one quality that all 63 of them had, they found that they were all **absorbed** in their occupations. Absorbed meaning they totally loved what they were doing, totally believed in what they were doing, and were hungry and passionate for success. None of these millionaires inherited their fortune, none were lottery winners. Many of them worked for several years without getting paid as they grew their businesses.

This now brings us to that part of the research that will help us get rid of excuses. Of these 63, 80% came from a blue collar background. There goes that excuse that you have to come from a well connected family. 68% did not have college degrees. Bye-bye higher degrees of education excuse, and this probably also takes care of the above average I.Q. and the good grades excuses. One more excuse to go. 47% were ugly ... only kidding. I just made this last one up. Other interesting statistics from this study were that on the average it took them 17 years to get to the millionaire status. So forget about quick fixes and get-rich-quick schemes. On the average they went personally bankrupt 2.7 times, so the need for being a risk taker with a good dose of determination and persistence certainly comes in handy.

Doing what you love, believing in what you're doing, hunger for success, and passion all lead to a commitment to excellence. I remember walking into a store and seeing this sign:

Excellence Can Be Attained If You . . .

Care more than others think is wise . . .
Risk more than others think is safe . . .
Dream more than others think is practical . . .
Expect more than others think is possible . . .

The best way to show that you care is to listen. Risk taking we know about already from this study, and we'll be discussing dreams when we get to goal setting. Dreams are goals with wings. Dreaming is something that keeps our souls alive; we always need to have dreams that we're reaching for. It's dreams that can really turn us on. After all Martin Luther King said, "I have a dream". He didn't say, "I have a strategic plan". Expectations will lead us to our third piece of the success foundation.

Goals

What is needed now is the balancing of attitudes, skills, absorption and **action**!

Focus! Attitude + Great Plans! Knowing where you're going to specifically direct your attention, and where you're going to follow-through.

Since this is a book on the goal achievement process, it should come as no surprise that the third quality of success is having a goal orientation. Making goal setting and goal achieving a daily, weekly, monthly habit, a way of life.

Part 2 is dedicated exclusively to this master skill. So for now we're just going to say that goal setting is the third part of what propels people forward. The goal achievement process in its full glory will be intimately covered in the next part.

The Glue

What minimizes our fears, bad habits and excuses are our skills, attitudes, absorption and goals. There is also the glue that holds together our positive attributes. We need a glue because the business of success does not happen overnight. These are the four ingredients of the glue, the glue that holds us together over the sometimes frustrating journey towards success, towards the use of our full potential.

I and II. **Determination and Persistence.** The twins. In an interview with Harrison Ford, the fabulously successful actor, he said that a large part of his success was not giving up. He was a carpenter for the first ten years of his striving to be a full time actor. He just kept getting on the audition bus. He noticed every two years or so that the people getting on the bus were a totally new group. All the others had given up. But he just kept showing up and improving his skills. I agree. A large part of your success is not giving up.

III. **A Sense of Humor... Fun!** If you're not having fun, is it worth it? I don't mean constant laughter and ecstasy, but I certainly don't mean debilitating stress and burn out that endangers your health.

To drive home this point about the importance of having a sense of humor, let's quote two great humorists. The first is Marx, no, not Karl. Not exactly the world's greatest humorist. Yes, that's right, Groucho. He said two things worth quoting here. "The other morning I shot an elephant in my pajamas. How it got in there I'll never know." The other one, "I would never join a country club that would have me as a member."

I love this last one because it reminds us to take what we do seriously, but not to take ourselves to seriously. Great advice.

The other great humorist is Allen. Gracie? Could be. Gracie Allen was married to George Burns and said that one of George's goals was to die young. And he accomplished this. He died 100 years young. We seem to have three ages; our chronological age, when we were born up to present day; our physical age; and our psychological age, how old we think we are. Well, George Burns certainly felt young. When asked why he didn't date women his own age, he said that there weren't any. Having the ability to laugh, especially the ability to laugh at ourselves and to make others laugh certainly keeps us young. Regarding our physical age, researchers have found that someone can be 35 years old with a heart or other organs of a 55 year old, and vice versa. Someone can be 55 with the heart of a 35 year old. It has something to do with how well, or how badly, we handle stress.

The Allen I was thinking of is Woody. Woody Allen said, "80% of success is showing up". The other 20% being ... on time, ready to go. Laugh a lot ... liberating, cleansing laughter.

IV. **High Self-Esteem.** See yourself as a worthwhile, valuable, contributing individual. There's an epidemic out there of low self-esteem which is the cause of much of the drug and alcohol abuse. When you see yourself as valuable you wouldn't even consider dumping drugs into your body. You wouldn't do anything to cloud up your clear consciousness.

Some people suffer from the "Popeye Syndrome" of, "I am what I am". They see themselves as miserable, tough SOB's, and say that there just isn't anything they can do about it because that's who they are. More excuses. People can change, and for the better. Better for them, better for their family, better for society.

One of the most powerful affirmations of a successful life came out of Henry David Thoreau's *Walden*. "As I advance confidently in the direction of my own dreams and endeavors, to live the life which I have imagined, and take the necessary risks, I will meet with success, unexpected in common hours."

So much said in a few lines. I have found this to be true of the successful people that I know. They tell me that life is so much more sweeter and fulfilling than they had ever hoped or dreamed possible . . . or had ever expected.

It is possible for all of us, in fact, it's our destiny, our birthright, to be fulfilled, to be using our full potential.

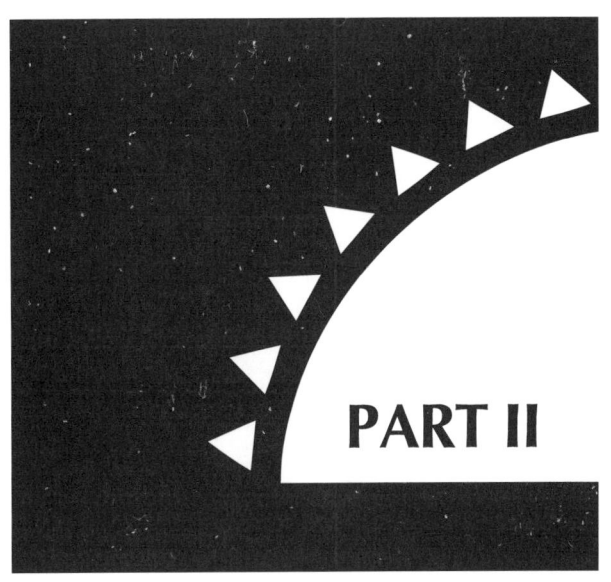

The Power of Goals

Chapter Four

The Goal Achievement Process (G.A.P.)

"Let's go to the video tape."

As in sports I'm going to use video, actually quotes from popular movies to help me drive home some of my points, using the principle that a picture is worth a thousand words. Sometimes the points that I want to get across may be a bit abstract, so the use of these familiar scenes can help you visualize what I'm trying to get across. Plus it will help you remember my message for a longer time, if not permanently. It's not unusual for me to be walking down a street, and someone will come up to me and say, "You look familiar." They won't remember my name, but eventually they'll get around to saying, "I attended one of your seminars several years back. You played that scene from such and such, and the message was . . . " After all these years they still remember the message, are still using the strategies to get results, and the film clip helped.

Before we go to our first clip here are some of my beliefs concerning the power of goal setting. Goal setting is a core, fundamental success strategy. It is something that is simple, practical, and immediately applicable. You can use it starting today, and you can use it for the rest of your life. It can have a very profound impact on your personal and professional success. Goal setting is a full potential tune-up.

Now, to the video. Remember that show *Name That Tune*? Where the moderator would say, "Can you name that tune in five notes?" and the contestants would say, "I can name that in four notes;" . . . "Three notes." Until someone went first. Well I'm going to give you one word! We're going to play *Name That Quote/Movie*. In one word? Yes, I believe that this quote is so famous that you may actually be able to name the quote, and the movie it's from in one word. In fact, this quote is so famous that you may never have seen, or even have heard of the movie that it is from, but you will still be able to name that quote. In one word? Well, with my seminar participants, when I would put up two words they would know it right away, 100% of the time. So, I decided to go to one word, which I admit is tough, but about 20% of my audiences still would get it in one word.

So, here's the one word: "I . . . "
Did you get it? Congrats, if you did, if not here's the second clue/ word: "I coulda . . . "

You definitely got it now, **"I coulda been somebody, I coulda been a contenda."**

You get extra credit if you named both the quote, and the movie, *On the Waterfront*.

And a tremendous amount of bonus points if you named the actors in the scene.

Two brothers sitting in the back seat of a car, Rod Steiger, the older brother, and Marlon Brando, the younger brother, giving up on himself so early in life.

What was holding Marlon back from being as successful as he could have been? When you watch the entire scene it's obvious that Terry Malloy (the character played by Brando) fell into some of the pitfalls that we discussed on what holds people back. He was blaming his brother ("It was you Charlie." [Rod Steiger's character]). He wasn't taking responsibility for his own success or failure, he was whining, and he did no planning. On the responsibility point, here's a phrase that reminds all of us who's ultimately in control of our success or failure. It's a 10 letter acronym, each letter representing a two letter word. **IIITBIIUTM** . . . 10 two letter words that make for a very powerful success reminder . . . **If It Is To Be It Is Up To Me**.

This scene reminds me of two things. One, that one of my objectives in writing this book was to help you to never have to look back on your life and say, "I coulda been a contenda, I coulda been somebody." Take the simple advice in this book, and you will definitely minimize the regrets in your life, and avoid getting into the coulda, shoulda, oughta emptiness. I mean, after all, what is it that people regret most, what they did, or yes, that's right, what they didn't do. The old truism, that the pain of discipline weighs ounces, while regret weighs tons. That's my objective for you, to help you minimize the regrets in your life, and maximize the successes.

If I had the opportunity to give Marlon's character some advice it would have been in the realm of planning. Planning was the way out of the valley of excuses and regrets for Malloy.

Experience The Power Of Planning

Here's a simple exercise I'm going to have you go through, to directly experience the power of planning, the power of planning in helping you to get better results.

Look at the page with the numbers on page 26, with the word **ACTION** at the top.

I want you to circle as many numbers as you can in one minute. But, before you start, here are two groundrules. One, you can not take your pen or pencil, put it at the top of the numbers, and then put one big circle around all of them at once. Some people would call this creativity, but in this game it's called cheating. The second rule is I want you to see how many numbers you can circle **consecutively**. Which means, you see the number 1 circled in the upper left hand corner, now find the number two, and circle it, then the number three and circle it, and so on for one minute. By the way, all the numbers are there, no tricks on my part, so I don't want you whining, "I can't find number seven, it's not here". They're all there, OK? Here's your one minute. Time it yourself, and . . . go!

Like most people you were probably able to circle anywhere between 12-29 numbers. When you take action you will get some results. But, were the results as high as they could have been? Were you busy **and** productive, or did you fall into the time trap of being busy without being effective? Yeah, I probably could have done a little better you're thinking, but I'm going to show you how you could have been a quantum leap better. Before I do, I want to make a few points about this exercise, and about taking action without planning. The one minute of circling numbers is analogous to how a lot of people run their lives. Busy, busy, busy. Running all over the place. In fact, running around like chickens with their heads cut off. Busy, busy, busy, and at the end of the day totally exhausted, fatigued, overwhelmed, crazed, and wondering, "But what have I accomplished?" Left with a big question mark in their minds. Like little Fievel Hamsterwitz. Ever watch those little hamsters on a wheel? The faster they go, the behinder they get.

I call this the Toody Muldoon approach to getting results in life. Some of you may remember Toody as the police officer in the TV show from the 60's, *Car 54, Where Are You*? He frequently would say, "Ooh, ooh."

Action

1 61 13 42 74 14
41 9 81 70 18 22
17 21 45 86 2 46
89 49 34 30
5 69 78 38 50
37 85 29 6 10
25 33 65 82 90
53 57 26 58
73 77 54 62
15 79 39 32 66 76 16
31 3 71 80 8 40
47 83 55
7 27 28 24 56
51 75 11 67 72 12 52 20
19 23 36 4
43 68 88 48
87 44
35 59 63 84 64 60

Plan

1 61 13 | 42 74 14

41 9 81 | 70 18 22

17 21 45 | 86 2 46

89 49 | 34 30

5 69 | 78 38 50

37 85 29 | 6 10

25 33 65 | 82 90

53 57 | 26 58

73 77 | 54 62 66

---

15 79 39 | 32 76 16

31 3 71 | 80 8 40

47 83 55 | 28 24 56

7 27 | 72 52

51 75 11 67 | 12 20 36 4

19 23 | 88

43 | 68 48

87 | 44

35 59 63 | 84 64 60

That's how a lot of people run their lives, "Ooh, maybe I'm interested in this, ooh, maybe I'm interested in that." Never taking the time to step back and plan. Just throwing themselves at the first thing that comes their way . . . the old and tired reactive approach. Yes, you will get some results this way, you can be successful in spite of yourself, just by taking action, by trying different things. In fact, it's healthy to do some experimenting, but you need to balance (ah, that concept again) it with planning. As you will experience now, planning will help you to use more of your potential, and help you to get the type of results that will really open your mind and heart to the power of planning.

Look at page 27. You'll see the same numbers schematic, but this time with the word **PLAN** at the top, and a vertical and a horizontal line. Next to the word **PLAN** put an = sign, and after the = sign write the word **investment**. Planning is an investment in yourself. People don't plan to fail, they fail to plan. Let me prove this to you, by giving out some new information before you take action.

When you look at the vertical line, what does it separate? The left side from the right side? Well, that's one right answer, but not the answer I was looking for. Yes, it separates the odd numbers from the even numbers. All of the odd numbers are on the left side, and all of the even numbers are on the right side. This will help you locate the number you're looking for that much quicker. Here's a second piece of new information. When you put a horizontal line in there it creates a quadrant, and this will help us to realize that there is a repeating pattern to the action we need to take. The pattern goes like this. Obviously the #1 is still in the upper left hand corner, now notice that the number 2 is in the upper right hand quadrant. Find it? Number 3 is in the lower left hand quadrant. Number 4 in the lower right hand quadrant. Then the pattern repeats itself with the number 5 being back in the upper left hand quadrant, number 6 in the upper right hand quadrant. There's the pattern. Now, knowing that there is a pattern to follow will help you to be more productive and more effective, meaning that in the one minute allotted you will experience circling more numbers. You'll still be busy, in fact, even busier, but you'll be productive. And the busyness won't be a draining exhausting busyness, but fulfilling, results-oriented action.

Ready? Here's your one minute. Get set, time the one minute, go!

Experience the difference? If you're like most of the people I have worked with the second round resulted in you circling anywhere from 20%-300% more numbers. 300%? Yes, circling 12 the first time, and 36 the second, as an example. By the way, the most numbers anyone that I know of has circled after the second round is 63. Just a little something to get your competitive juices flowing.

Guaranteed Results

When you take the time to plan, to gather more information, to find out about possible patterns, strategies, techniques that you can use, by doing "your homework," by setting goals before just plowing ahead, **your results will be greater. Guaranteed.** I do guarantee greater results for you by making goal setting a part of your life, by making it a daily, weekly, monthly, quarterly, annual and for the rest of your life habit.

The Two Pains

There are two pains in life, the pain of discipline, and the pain of regret. Which one will you choose? By experiencing the pain of discipline, which weighs ounces, and is a simple and easy discipline to learn and do, you will minimize the pain of regret. By not disciplining yourself, taking the time to set goals, you will experience the pain of regret, which weighs tons.

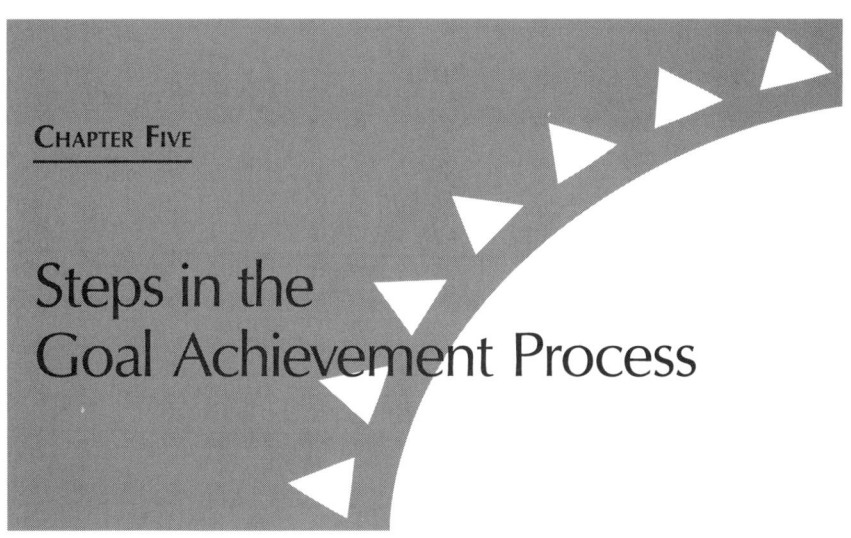

CHAPTER FIVE

Steps in the Goal Achievement Process

The 5 W's & The 1 H—What We Will Be Covering

Who? . . . You! My entire focus is on you. Helping you to achieve greater and greater personal and professional success.

What? . . . Goal setting, a core, fundamental, back to the basics, success skill. It's been said that goals = success, and success = goals, and all the rest is commentary. People don't plan to fail. They just fail to plan.

Focus

Think of me as your designated goal achievement coach. One of the things I will be coaching you on is how to have greater focus and clarity in your life. But what is focus? What does it mean to you to be a focused individual? You might be thinking: Someone with definite of purpose, the ability to stick to one thing, single-mindedness, the ability to block everything out and concentrate. All of these have to do with focus. Let me share with you something I heard from an interview with Bob Wolfe of Boston, the first "Super Agent" for professional athletes. One of Bob's first super star athletes was Larry Bird, the famous basketball player for the Boston Celtics. When Bob was asked to describe what made Larry Bird so special, here were the qualities he mentioned:

- Single-mindedness of Purpose
- Mental Toughness

- Unusual Self-Discipline
- Extraordinary Commitment
- Preparation *More* Than Anyone Else

Several years back I was walking with an insurance executive, and we were talking about some of the successful people in his company. He said something that I will never forget, "When I think of Roy, I think of somebody who's really focused." I jumped right on this great opportunity and asked him what he meant by focus. He said, "He knows what he wants. He knows how to get it, and he takes action on what it is that he wants." A truly simple definition of what it means to be focused. A focused individual is someone who:

- knows what he wants
- knows how to get it, and
- takes action!

I believe you need all three to be focused. I have met some people who know what they want, but they're still not focused. I have met people who know what they want, know how to get it, and are still not focused. You need all three parts to be focused. The third piece is what I call **The Nike Factor**. From Nike's corporate philosophy made known to us through their ads, **Just Do It!**

But, maybe I'm getting too abstract here. So what do we do when we start to get too abstract? That's right, "We go to the video."

When I go to the movies I don't consciously look for these transcendental scenes, those scenes that have a universally appealing message, and "funnily" enough also happen to be the most entertaining. I just sit there enjoying the movie, and suddenly a particular scene will just move and wash over me, and I'll think, "Voila, eureka, here's a scene that I can use." This thrill of discovery is extremely satisfying.

When it comes to focus, far and away, the best example I have ever come across in helping us to get a clearer understanding of what it means to be focused, is the famous finger scene from *City Slickers*.

Mitchy the Kid played by Billy Crystal, and Curly played by Jack Palance are riding their horses together, when Mitch says, "See, now that's great, your life makes sense to you." Curly laughs, says a few words, and then bestows upon Billy this phenomenal wisdom, "None of you get it. Do you know what the secret to life is?"

- ◆ Mitch: "No, what?"
- ◆ Curly: "This." — as he holds up his index finger.

- Mitch: "Your finger?" being a wise guy New Yorker.
- Curly: "One thing, just one thing, you stick to that, and everything else don't mean s_ _ _ ."
- Mitch: "That's great, but what's the one thing?"
- Curly: "That's what you gotta figure out."

That is what focused individuals have been able to figure out—what that one thing is that they can totally commit to, totally absorb themselves in for the betterment of themselves, their family, their company and their society. It is the organizing principle of their lives ... if you will, their purpose, their mission. It is clear, meaningful (to you) goals that inevitably, over a time period that is different for everybody, lead to vision, purpose and mission in life. Oh, my one thing is that I help people set and achieve goals. See the focus flow chart on page 34 for another way of looking at the direction that goal setting can take you. This is what we will be giving you guidelines for in this chapter.

Why? ... Why bother to invest the time to set goals?

It's a sad fact that most people will spend more time planning a party, a weekend, than they do planning their lives. So why should people plan?

The Classic Study On Goals

If I had 100,000 seminar participants attention at one time (which is not a goal of mine yet, but with distance learning technology it will be a goal of mine soon), and I asked them, "By a show of hands, how many of you believe that having goals is important?" What percent would raise their hands? If you said 100 percent, you said the same amount that I would have said. I believe that almost everybody, if not everybody, believes that goals are important. Now, if I then asked them this follow-up question, "By a show of hands, how many of you have goals that are written down?" What percent would be able to raise their hands now?

Let's talk about the classic study on goal setting which will give us insight into how many of these 100,000 would probably still have their hands up.

The study was a 20 year study conducted by Yale University. The researchers wanted to study what motivates people and the role that goals play in motivation. The study was started in 1953 with the researchers working with that year's graduating class. First they asked all the graduating seniors if they believed that goals were important to help one to be more successful. Surprise, 100 percent said that goals were important. Then the researchers asked the se-

Focus!

Goals: Written and Visible

Priorities

Organization

Execution

Accountability: Coaching and Fine Tuning

BREAKTHROUGH RESULTS: Exceeding Goals and Quotas

Increased Sales, Income and Job Satisfaction

Focus Flow Chart

niors three questions very specific to goals. The three questions were 1) Do you have goals? 2) Do you write them down? 3) Do you have a plan for their accomplishment? What percent of these graduating seniors were able to say yes to all three questions? If you guessed three percent, you were correct. Less than one out of twenty were able to say yes to all three questions.

The researchers also found that 12 percent did indeed have goals, but they didn't write them down. I meet people like this all the time. They say to me I have goals but I don't write them down. More about these people later when we look at a second study on goal achievement. The other 85 percent? They came up with a resounding, as my daughters would say, "Duh". The best that they could offer up as goals were favorites like, "I want to be happy". "I want to be healthy". And of course that all time favorite, "I want to be rich!" These are not goals. These are common wishes and fantasies of everybody.

The fact that only 3 percent had written goals with action plans is not the moral or the power of this study though. Let's go 20 years up to 1973 to look at what happened to the group that had written goals when compared to the other two groups. Oh, by the way, every study that I have read on goal setting always tags the number of people who actually have written goals with plans at 1-5 percent. So, this study is right in the middle. We can comfortably say that in our culture 1-5 percent of people have written goals with written plans for their accomplishment.

At the end of the twenty years the researchers asked the surviving members of the class of '53 several questions. Many of them were very subjective, asking them about the quality of their home and work relationships, how they liked their jobs, questions of this nature. The one question that we will zero in on was objective and measurable. They asked them what their financial net worth was. Here it is twenty years later. Just write down what your net worth is. What they found was astounding. Many times, the one fact from my workshops that the participants tell their friends about is the results from this one question. The researchers found that the 3 percent who had written goals with action plans that were implemented over the twenty years had a financial net worth **more than the other 97 percent combined**! That's right. If you added up the net worth of the 3 percent and added up the net worth of the other 97 percent, the net worth of the 3 percent was higher. The 3 percent also scored very well on the subjective side of the questions, keeping with our challenge of having balance in life.

They found some interesting things out about these 3 percent. They found that some of them did have above average I.Q.'s, excellent grades, well connected families, but they also found that many of them were in the bottom half of the class, had average I.Q.'s and did not come from privileged families. Keeping right in line with the other research that helped us get rid of myths and excuses.

On the average, the 3 percent had written goals, starting in 1953 for one, two, three, five, ten and twenty years. They had literally written down what their earning goals were for 1953, 1954, 1955, 1958 and so on. When we get to the how to's of goal setting we will discuss the importance of keeping goals flexible, and this group exhibited this as well. Just because they wrote down specific income and net worth goals didn't mean they couldn't change them. The researchers concluded that the writing down of goals played a major part in their successful goal achievement, and with regard to the study's over all research into motivation, it was concluded that written goals play a major part in motivation.

The difference between those who write down their goals and those who choose to just carry them around in their head? A one year study following those who write down their goals, and those who do not write them down, found that those who did, accomplished 50 percent more of their goals than those who didn't.

Don't Think It, Ink It

Writing something down is all about making commitments. When you write something down it drives your commitment to accomplish it deeper. Your resolve is stronger. You persist in the face of frustrations and obstacles.

Why should you make goal setting a lifetime habit?

- Gives you direction in life
- A target to shoot for
- Something to measure your success against
- A greater sense of accomplishment and achievement
- Gives you a reason to wake up in the morning
- Gives you a sense of purpose
- Greater balance in life
- Greater personal and professional fulfillment

These are just a few of the many excellent reasons for you to commit to a goal achievement program.

Why Don't People Set Goals?

So, now that we know why it is in our best interest to set goals, let's discuss something that's a little more difficult to answer. **Why don't people set goals**? 100 percent, or close to it, believe that goals are important. They can quite easily come up with a wonderful list of the benefits of goal setting, probably know of some friends who have benefited greatly from it, may even have heard about research on the powerful results one can expect from making it a practice, but they still do not take the time to write down goals for themselves. Why? I heard it said that one of the most difficult things you will do in your life is to sit down in front of a blank piece of paper and think. I guess so, judging from the fact that only 1-5 percent of people actually do have written goals.

Typically, when I ask why don't people set goals, the answers I get are: "It's too hard. It takes too much time. I don't know how. I'm afraid to. I'm too lazy." As you will find out from reading this book and using what you have learned, goal setting is easy. It doesn't take a lot of time. You will definitely learn a K.I.S.S. system on how to set goals, and there is absolutely nothing to be afraid of. Regarding people who are lazy, my own philosophy is that there really aren't any lazy people, just people who are experiencing some difficulty with low energy or focusing their energy. Have you ever met somebody at work who just seems to be lazy? But when you see them outside of work involved with something they really enjoy, here's this same "lazy" person running all over the place, having a great time and leading other people?

Here are some of the reasons I have come upon to answer why people don't set goals.

They really don't understand the importance. Another interesting bit of information came out of the Yale study. The researchers were asked if there was anything particular about the 3 percent who were so dedicated to the goal process. Was there anything that motivated them to have this deep commitment to the planning process? What they came up with has far-reaching implications. Their answer: **The conversation around the dinner table.** They had grown up in families that encouraged and believed in the goal setting, the planning process. They had parents who understood the value of taking the time to dream and plan and take action on your ideals.

I know for myself, looking forward to sitting down with my family for dinner was always something I enjoyed and looked forward to. I can still hear my father saying, "I love this time of day. This is my favorite time." Having dinner together was a regular thing. Sitting together and sharing what went on during the day and talking about what we were working on and what we were doing to make it happen. Now, I said what the researchers said on this matter was profound because when you look at today's life styles, how often do families actually get together to eat, and more importantly, spend some time together?

Well, a recent public announcement has a famous actor advising families to spend at least one night a week together. One night? And he was saying it as if it was some revolutionary idea, or something that he knew might be difficult to do, but it was important enough to set as a goal, regardless of how difficult it might be to actually have it happen. The goal of getting together once a week. Sad.

People are always asking me if I teach my two children to set goals. As we know all too well, the best way to teach our children is by example. So I don't talk to my children about goals too much . . . directly. If they knew that I wanted them to and that it was important to me that they regularly set goals, there's a good chance that they would rebel and learn to hate goals because it's something their parents made them do. But indirectly, my family is surrounded by the message of goals. Certainly they know that I give seminars on goal setting and time management. They see me writing out my own goals. I drop hints in our conversations about how goals can help people, and whenever they come into my office, my goals are posted everywhere. So yes, they get the message, and quite clearly know that I support and encourage them to set goals for themselves. They know that we will be there for them when they need help and coaching on their goals.

Many people who raise their hands and say that goals are important really don't get it. They're probably just following the crowd, saying that goals are important because everybody else says they're important. But the three percent who do set goals understand in their brain and in their veins, in their minds and in their hearts, that goals make a difference, that goals are a non-negotiable part of their lives. Non-negotiable meaning that it's a habit, a way of life, just like breathing in and breathing out.

They were never taught how. Read this question very carefully. In your formal classroom training, anywhere from first to twelfth grade, did you receive any classroom instruction on how to set goals? Rarely in my workshops do more than two people raise their hands. Our educational system just doesn't teach this subject. Oh yes, perhaps they do mention goals, and probably even have some neat, colorful posters about the power of goals. But as far as actually teaching you how to do it, and that it's a process, very few people have received training on how to set and achieve goals. If, during first to twelfth grade, you did receive any training, it was usually the kind of training you went out and got on your own from a book, audiotape, videotape or seminar you signed up for out of your own motivation to better yourself.

Even people with 4 years of college and beyond, all the way up to a doctorate, still cannot raise their hands when asked if they received any classroom training on goal setting. Unbelievable! But hope springs eternal. My daughters have been coming home since sixth grade with these personal planning organizers that are handed out at the beginning of the year. Some really motivational stuff is written in there. I've even quoted some of the material in my seminars. Fortunately these are being distributed; unfortunately there is no training on how to use them. But someday soon, I believe it will happen. No, I haven't written down as a goal for myself to be the one to carry forward this message to the public and private schools, but perhaps someday. Right now, it is not a burning desire within me. Obviously, the future can change, regarding my calling in this field.

The more "advanced" colleges and universities are starting to offer these classes. What I have heard referred to as "Life Skills" courses. Classes on goal setting, time management, selling skills, presentation skills, negotiation skills and how to balance a checkbook skills. All the kind of things unfortunately we have to wait for until we're out of school to start learning. It's certainly good and encouraging news that our educational system is starting to come awake on these all important subjects.

In a few chapters from now I will teach you a very simple and effective way to set goals. No longer will you have to say or whine, "I don't know how to set goals". This next excuse is a biggee.

They feel they already are successful or can be successful without having to set goals. You know what? You can be successful without ever having written down a goal, and I do meet people who are successful who are not into goals. But they are definitely the exception to the rule. I am not saying that you can't be successful without goals, but I am saying that by making goal setting a way of life, you greatly increase the odds of creating a life that you are truly proud of.

There is a great quote attributed to too many people for me to know who actually said it. It is, "The best way to predict the future is to create it." That's what goal setting does for you. It helps you to create your future. It helps you make clearer and more powerful decisions about the direction in which you want to take your life.

I have also met some people whom I would call "successful failures." People who accomplished a lot in a chosen field, but measured their success by the guidelines of others. Winning contests, beating quotas, getting promotions, but knowing within themselves that they never came close to their true potential. Sure, they are called successful by other people's standards, but what about the standards that they never set for themselves? Never knowing just how high they could have gone.

Now, for the biggest reason why people don't set goals. We'll discuss it in two parts.

Fear of rejection, the fear of criticism. Do you enjoy being criticized, ridiculed, rejected, being embarrassed, and appearing foolish? The answer is obvious . . . "Not!" The #1 reason why people don't set goals is **FEAR**. Here's public enemy #1 again. Remember fear's role when we were discussing what holds people back? We come back to fear again. We learn about fear, and how it's associated with criticism and rejection early in life.

I'm sure this happened to all of us at least once in our adolescence. We're excited about something, something we're going to do, something we want to be, and what do we hear from our friends, "That's stupid. Who do you think you are? You can't do that." It's like a dagger, an arrow, going straight through your heart. It hurts badly. Hurts so badly that too often we listen to our hurtful, but well meaning friends, decide they're right and drop our plans, figuring it's much easier and safer to just go along with the crowd.

This happened to me when I was in third grade. I remember it as if it was yesterday. Mrs. Streeter was going around the class asking each of my classmates that core third grade question, "What do you want to be when you grow up?" When she came to me, I had no doubt to how I was going to answer that question. I proudly and assertively gave my answer, and here was her immediate response, "That's stupid!" The pain in my chest is still there. I was devastated. You're probably wondering what did I say? Well, that's not the point. See, I'm still protecting myself from any further ridicule. The point is that I believed in what I wanted, and was crushed. Eight years old and my dreams were already being trampled on. It's tough enough to answer this question, let alone without adding into the equation the fear of how people will respond to your answer.

This type of scenario also plays out in adulthood all to often. You're really excited about something, perhaps a new business venture, and from everywhere, all of these well meaning friends and family are coming up with all the reasons why you shouldn't or couldn't do it. This is why high self-esteem is so critical for success in life. Yes, you listen to what they have to say, you objectively consider their suggestions, you integrate what is valuable advice, and then you make your decision. Be careful not to just say to yourself,

"Oh, it's easier to do nothing. They're probably right." And there you are left with that low potential comfort zone again.

The fear of failure. The biggest reason why people don't set goals. Let me give you some advice:

- Understand that failure is indispensable to success.
- Learn to be in the habit of doubling your failure rate.
- Fail forward. Learn from your mistakes.

Several stories will help me drive home these points. Instead of going to the video, we're going to the story.

The classic has to do with a gentleman who lived in my hometown of West Orange, New Jersey for 37 years, around the turn of the century. One newspaper reporter was calling Mr. Thomas A. Edison the greatest failure of all time. Our story centers around a conversation between Mr. Edison and this young reporter. I first heard about this story from an account by the author Napoleon Hill. The same Napoleon Hill commissioned by Andrew Carnegie to write a book on success, *Think and Grow Rich*, by interviewing the great entrepreneurs of that time. Napoleon Hill met Thomas Edison and asked him to tell him about a meeting that he had had with a reporter.

Edison told Hill that the reporter had asked if it were true that he had done over 5,000 experiments trying to get the incandescent lightbulb to work. Edison said it was true, and that they still didn't have it solved. Well the reporter than said, "Why don't you quit? Obviously you have failed!" To which Edison immediately responded, "I haven't failed, I have found over 5,000 ways it won't work!" The story continues that Edison did over 11,000 experiments before he finally got the lightbulb to work. Napoleon Hill asked him how he finally got it to work. Edison's reply, "I ran out of ways it wouldn't work." Failure is indispensable to success.

I learned about doubling your failure rate from Tom Watson, the legendary founder of IBM. His advice to his employees, double your failure rate. Take more and more calculated risks. If you're working on something and you're having difficulty with it, don't cower and whine. Just make more attempts at solving the problem. This is tied into the third piece of advice. Fail forward; learn from your mistakes. Quite often after one of my talks, someone will come up to me and thank me for reminding him that some of his greatest successes came on the heels of what he considered, at the time, a failure. But he looked at the situation objectively, looked at it from a different perspective. "What are the lessons I can learn from this experience?" He moved forward from there, looking back at it now as a turning point in enjoying and getting more out of life. A solid foundation for future successes.

Failure can serve you

Two great lessons came out of one of my workshops. We were talking about the double-edged sword of the fear of failure. The theme was, if you fear failure enough, you will fail, figuring that the fear will immobilize you from taking the necessary action for success. I asked the question, "If you fear failure too much, what will happen?" The response I usually get is that you will fail, but at this seminar someone said you will **succeed**. Now, the fact that this person was a huge success story at this company really caught my attention. I asked her what she meant. She said that she is so afraid of failure, she takes whatever action is necessary to assure herself that there is no way she is going to fail. Interestingly, the fear of failure is motivating her to do what she knows she needs to do to be successful. The audience pretty much agreed with her. Quite a few other people chimed in with their own stories of how they make fear work for them.

The other story centers around the **prove-it factor**. Simply stated, "I didn't know I could do that until you told me that I couldn't." Something happens that kicks into high gear the motivation to prove to someone that he is wrong. Here's a classic story that will help make this point clear. At the workshop one of the attendees was a world class bike rider. He has traveled all over the world on bike trips. This trip was in Northern England and the hills were brutal. The two people on this trip were going to a city and weren't sure of how to get there or how far they were from the city. They saw someone on the road and asked for directions. The gentleman was very helpful, pointed them in the right direction, and then said something that proved to be a great lesson for all of us, "The hills are quite steep going that way, **you'll never be able to do it**." Their resolve skyrocketed. He said that those hills were the toughest he had ever climbed. He painted a beautiful picture by saying that they were like going up an elevator shaft. Every time either of them was ready to quit, he heard this man's voice saying, "You can't do it." They did it. They made it to the city without once having to stop to get off their bikes because the hills were too tough. He admitted that without that gentleman's challenge they would have definitely gotten off of their bikes and walked the steepest parts. A wonderful example of how to make challenges and tough situations work for you.

Author Larry Wilson in his book, *The Changing Game, Selling in the 90's*, interviewed the top 25 salespeople from 25 different industries. He defined top as someone who indeed was a top income earner, but not necessarily number one. The other criteria was that he loved what he was doing. He uncovered in these 25 successful salespeople seven strategic thinking patterns. The number one strategic thinking pattern, **"I cannot fail, I can only learn and grow."** A great message and strategy for all of us.

We all have fears, even the super successful, but they have learned ways to minimize their fears, just as you are learning. One of the most common bits of advice given to minimize fear is . . . **"Do the thing you fear and the death of fear is certain."** Balance planning with doing, and the death of fear **is** certain.

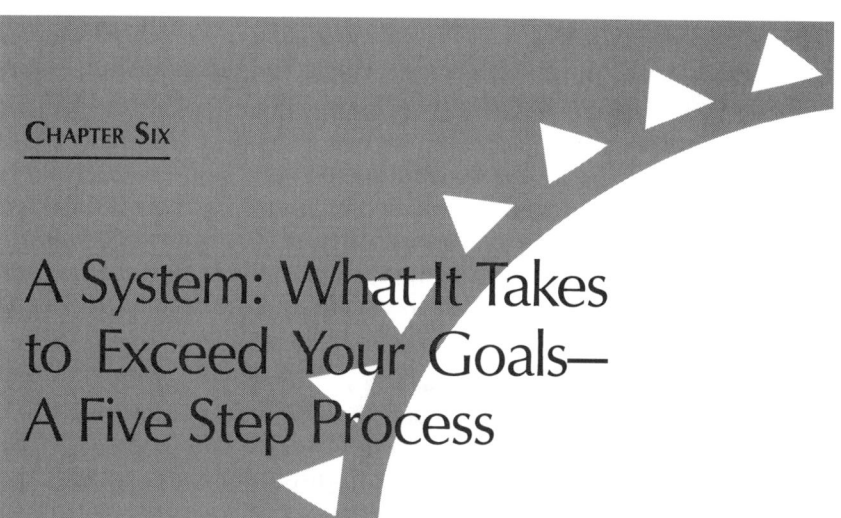

CHAPTER SIX

A System: What It Takes to Exceed Your Goals— A Five Step Process

It All Starts With Desire

A good friend of mine video taped the entire 1992 Winter Olympics. Good move, because he was able to record a five minute segment that is one of the most profound, moving and motivational stories I have ever seen.

It's about Bonnie Blair, and it's about our first step in the goal achievement process: **DESIRE**.

The segment is called, "The Making of A Champion" and is narrated by Charles Kuralt. It tracks Bonnie Blair's quest and accomplishment of winning five gold medals, from her fifth medal back to her first, going back to her childhood.

The main message from Bonnie is, "I love skating." And she needs to love skating because of the tremendous sacrifices she had to make regarding practice, practice, practice. One segment shows her waking up before 6 in the morning, smiling, even though she knows she is going to be spending the whole day skating. The other message is that Bonnie was born to do this, that she was almost literally born with skates on her feet. She had the perfect combination of an environment, her family, supporting and encouraging her to passionately pursue her love for skating, and she had the inner talent and drive/motivation to do whatever it takes (W.I.T.), and whatever is necessary (W.I.N.). Again, the two key ingredients of success, balancing skill with attitude. In this case, we're going to call attitude by another name, desire. Desire simply means, **"How badly** do you want it!" plus, "Are you willing to make the necessary sacrifices of hard work and study?"

Another great scene from a movie was in Rocky 3, when Clubber Lang, played by Mr. T, had no doubts about what he wanted. Very early in the opening scene you hear Lang saying, "I want Balboa, I want Balboa." No doubt he knew exactly what he wanted. He knew Curly's, "One thing, just one thing." He had the necessary focus . . . a tremendous, passionate, hungry, driven desire for success . . . no matter what.

Now some of you may be thinking, "But focus like this doesn't sound very healthy. It sounds like this can lead a person towards a miserable, unbalanced life." You might even know someone who had this kind of focus, and it lead to nothing but unhappiness and frustration. I know someone who was driven to be a radio announcer, so driven that the rest of his life suffered and led to a divorce. I know his ex-wife, and she said she couldn't stand his obsession. It was too all-consuming. Well, you know how I feel about balance. Yes, this kind of obsession can lead to unhappiness, but it doesn't have to. I also know plenty of excellent role models who were able to have it all. Tremendous success personally and professionally. They were able to balance their obsession by keeping perspective on the other opportunities for joy in life. But it doesn't just fall into your lap. You have to plan and focus your obsession. You have to plan for a balanced life. Careful of the excuse, "You can't have it all." I believe that you can.

Desire, a burning desire, is the starting point of all achievement, and as we'll later see, the ending point as well. Success begins and ends with desire. Desire is pure potentiality. I have heard it said that nature is not cruel, that we would not have these desires, unless the capacity, the ability to achieve these desires wasn't already there within us. Where there's a will there's a way. How badly do you want it?

Step II: Belief

The first two steps in the goal achievement process are attitudinal. First, desire. Second, belief. Back to the four aces of success, the four aces of belief. The belief that we will be emphasizing in this step is belief in yourself. Being able to wrap your mind around your desire, and believing deep within your mind, heart and gut that you can make it happen.

As Ralph Waldo Emerson said, "Nothing great was ever accomplished without enthusiasm." When you look at the word enthusiasm, you can make the last four letters into a powerful goal achievement reminder. The acronym for I.A.S.M. is, **I am sold myself**. Where does the first sale have to be made? To yourself. The most important sale is selling yourself on the belief that your goal, dream, vision, mission will happen for you and realizing the responsibility of success is contained in this ten, two letter word sentence. I.I.I.T.B.I.I.U.T.M. = **If It Is To Be It Is Up To Me**.

Belief, faith, and conviction. The faith that you saw in *Indiana Jones, The Last Crusade*. Indy's father (Sean Connery) had just been shot, and his only hope for survival was contained in an elixir that Indy (Harrison Ford) had to get, but it was on the other side of a wide chasm. Indy looked down the deep cliff, looked across the wide chasm and said, "It's impossible. Nobody can jump this." Then you hear his father say, "You must believe boy, you must believe." Indy knows it's impossible, but he can do it because the leap is a leap of faith. He closes his eyes, puts his hand over his heart, extends one of his feet, leans forward, and miraculously there is a stone bridge, unseen to his eye from the vantage point he had, that allows him to cross the chasm and to attain his goal—which ultimately does save his father's life. His one step is a clear metaphor for our starting our own journey towards success. And like his first step, our first step is also the most difficult to take. As the Chinese proverb goes, a thousand mile journey begins with one step. Many times it's also the toughest step to take. I know that in starting this book the toughest part was writing down those first few words. But once you do discipline yourself, and just get started, you rapidly pick up momentum, and your belief, faith and conviction, meaning no doubt, deepen.

Concerning no doubt, I'm not saying that you never have a thought or a mood that crosses your mind that contains doubt. What I am saying is that your overall attitude is one of deep conviction. If you want something bad enough and long enough, you do believe that it will be yours. You have learned the profound habit of not paying too much attention to these self-limiting beliefs and moods. You treat them like you would treat a passing cloud. You see it, but you don't get caught up in it. Eventually it just passes by, leaving you with your deep resolve for success.

STEP III: *WRITE IT DOWN!*

DON'T THINK IT INK IT!!!

Put think to ink. This separates the top performers from the mediocre performers. Remember the 3 percent in our study who achieved the greatest results and accomplished 50 percent more of their goals over a year's time than the 12 percent who carry them around in their head without writing them down? To transform a dream into reality, write the dream down on paper. A simple success formula is decide what you want and write it down.

Speaking of simple let's now learn the K.I.S.S. method of writing down goals. I first learned that it is S.M.A.R.T. to set goals from listening to an audiocassette program by Ken Blanchard, the author of *The One Minute Manager*. In the audio program Ken explained the different parts of S.M.A.R.T. goals. This is Part I of how to write goals.

S = Specific

Specificity = Predictability. The more specific your goals, the more predictable it is that they will be achieved. Fuzzy goals = fuzzy results. In a moment I'm going to have you go through an exercise that will help you set goals in specific categories.

Success is in the details. When Jack Welch, the CEO of General Electric, was asked what the secret was to his success, he answered, "A fanatical attention to detail." I'll help you set **"Mission Goals."** For example, I get the XYZ contract, as well as the all important **"How to Goals."** The details are the action steps that will lead to achieving the mission goal. For example, I get an appointment with XYZ's Vice President, that generates a proposal addressing their specific needs. Remember our definition of focus, "I know what I want," (mission goals) "I know how to get it," (how to goals) and "I take action."

When I ask people what their goals are, too often I hear, "I want to be happy." "I want to be healthy." "I want to be rich." These are not goals. These are wishes and fantasies that we all have. The pursuit of being healthy, wealthy and wise. What you need to do is break these general statements down into what achievements will make you happy, what disciplines/habits will get you healthy, and what you specifically mean by rich. What is your plan to get rich?

M = Measurable and Motivational

Another bit of wisdom I learned from management books is **what gets measured gets managed, gets done**. You can't mange it effectively if you can't measure it. A lot of people say, "My job can't be measured." A management guru's answer to that? "Well, I guess we don't need your job then."

My own experience with measurable goals is if my goals are not specific and measurable, it causes a lot of confusion and frustration at the end of the month when I want to see how I'm doing with my goals. I would look at the goals and scratch my head, wondering if I had hit them? Was I far off from hitting them? What did I have to do to self-correct? Without the goals being specific and measurable the whole goal achievement process was thrown off its foundation. Too often frustration can lead to this kind of conclusion, "Oh well, this goal setting stuff doesn't work anyway. Why bother?" They quit before they really give it a chance. With this goal achievement system **I guarantee results**! Guaranteed results if you give it at least six months and get the necessary coaching. What will happen over time is that your goals do get more and more specific. They do get more and more measurable. The whole process picks up tremendous momentum. I believe that you raise the predictability, the probability of achieving your goals by 50 percent, just by having your goals specific and measurable. I believe that these two qualities alone are the very foundation of a powerful goal achievement system. This is why the role of the coach is so critical. One of the first jobs of your coach is to help you get your goals specific and measurable. From there everything else can be built upon. Unfortunately, regarding coaching, too often it's the blind leading the blind. When we get to the "Schwarzenegger Effect" we'll spend time helping the coaches to coach effectively.

M also stands for **motivational**. Very simply, this means that your goals have to turn you on. You're crystal clear on that great acronym, W.I.I.F.M? What's in it for me? Crystal clear on the benefits and results that you get from the accomplishment of your goals. Crystal clear on the benefits to you, your family, your place of work, and your community-at-large. Balance once again. Not a selfish W.I.I.F.M. but an understanding that charity does begin at home and then does extend out.

Reasons help us with our motivation. The more reasons we have for achieving our goals, the more motivation it will generate. If you have one or two reasons you want to accomplish something, it will give you some motivation, but when you have 30, 40, 50 or more reasons to hit your goals, your motivation will be unstoppable.

Everyone has his own personal reasons why he wants what he wants. Some examples might be higher self-esteem, to be able to give more to one's family and to one's community, to be happier, to have a greater sense of accomplishment and fulfillment, to have more time for oneself, to be able to travel the world carefree, and on and on. Take the time to do the exercise on reasons, on page 51, to generate for yourself the kind of resolve that confidently moves you towards your goals.

A = Attainable

People are always asking me, "Mark, should I set my goals high, or should I set my goals low?" My answer is, "Yes." Meaning just do it. Don't over analyze. Stay away from that old nemesis called paralysis by analysis. To give you a bit more guidance than just yes, let me give you a rule of thumb concerning how you set your goals. Since belief is an important part of our goal achievement system, I suggest that you set goals that you can wrap your mind around, goals that you believe are realistic and attainable for you. Then whatever that level is, put some stretch into it. It's like an exercise I see motivational speakers use, and use effectively, to get this point across. Raise your hand. Now raise it as high as it can go. Now have it go another 1/4 of an inch higher. Amazing isn't it? Everybody can always go a little bit higher. Same with your goals. Set them high, then stretch. As the poet Robert Browning said, "A person's reach should exceed his grasp, or what's a heaven for?" Great advice for goal setting.

Some speakers recommend that you set outrageously high goals. They say, "Shoot for the moon, and if you miss it, you'll still hit the stars." Because of the belief factor, I suggest that you don't set outrageously high goals at first. My experience with the goal process is that over time your goals do get higher and higher, and what might have been an outrageously high goal a short while ago is now a very attainable stretch goal.

I think that our own experiences with managers who set goals too high bears out the logic of how high to set our goals. Too often managers will set outrageously high goals that can totally demotivate the troops. Everyone's thinking, "No way. There's just no way that I can hit these goals." This type of thinking leads to half-hearted efforts and self-fulfilling prophecies of underachievement.

Some managers do set irresponsible, poorly thought out goals and quotas. But remember the balance factor here. Some wise managers have come across people who are "successful failures," doing more than all right, but operating way below their and the company's potential. This is where the analysis does pay off. The manager sees tremendous opportunity, knows that with the proper focus and with consistent, constructive coaching, he will show the team that these goals are realistic and attainable. This is when truly wonderful breakthrough results can become reality. This is the beauty of the goal achievement process. It is both a science and an

The Reasons Why I Want to Achieve My Goals

The more reasons you have, the more you will be motivated.

-
-
-
-
-
-
-

NOTE: Make up additional sheets. Go for 30, 40, 100 reasons why you want, need, *must* achieve your goals.

art. Rules are to be broken, and rules are to be kept. The process teaches us when and where.

R = Relevant

Those activities that will get you the greatest results. Having the **wisdom** to know and the **courage** to do those activities that will be of the highest impact. Those activities that will get you the greatest return on your investment of time and energy.

This is where your coach can help you the most. By being clear about these activities, you start to minimize and eventually eliminate being busy without being productive. Not knowing your relevant activities is the greatest cause of being like a chicken running around with its head cut off. Moving away from being diffused to being focused, and focused on the right things. Making sure that you're not charging ahead, full steam, in the wrong direction.

I was traveling in a car with my father-in-law on Route 9 South. There was no traffic on our side, but the other side was jammed bumper to bumper for quite a distance. I suddenly realized that we were going the wrong way and said, "Joe, we have to take 9 North." He said, "I know, but we're making such great time." That's how, unfortunately, too many people run their lives, going fast in the wrong direction. The faster they go the behinder they get.

This holds true for teams as well. When everybody is clear on their relevant activities they will all pull in the same direction, instead of running all over the place, just creating activity and getting in each others way.

How do you start to make sure that you're involved in relevant activities? Very easy, just start. Take a pen or pencil and write down as many things as come to mind using the form we have provided on page 53. At the top of the form you will see the words,

> **How I plan to increase/impact productivity.**
> **Where I need to set goals.**

Now, take about five minutes and write down as many things as come to mind that fit into the category of high impact, doing what counts activities. Use the brainstorming rules of going for quantity of ideas, while shutting off your critical mind. At this point don't worry if you're writing down the right activities or not. Use your current situation as your barometer, your current business situation. Just write down what you believe will help you to be more

How I Plan to Increase/Impact Productivity Where I Need to Set Goals Make It Account/Individual Specific Where Possible

effective, more productive. For now, we're putting our attention on business goals. Later we'll set our personal goals.

Step II is to show this list to your coach. All your coach needs to do is let you know what you need to add, delete, fine-tune or reprioritize. The third step, in getting your goals relevant, is what brings us to the "T" in S.M.A.R.T.

T = Time frames and trackable

A goal needs a time frame. Without a time frame your goals merely remain wishes and fantasies. Think of your time frame as a lifeline, not a deadline. A lifeline because it infuses life into your days. Every day having a purpose, every day moving you closer and closer to your goals. Work with your coach on setting realistic time frames. Go through each of your goals and set the appropriate time frame for that goal. Keep in mind that there is no such thing as an unrealistic goal. Most of us set very aggressive time frames. We get so excited about the goal that perhaps we set up an overly ambitious accomplishment date. So here's the attitude I recommend you take regarding overly aggressive time lines. If the time frame has come and gone, and you haven't yet hit your goal, but this goal remains important in your overall plan for continued success, just move up the time frame. There are no unrealistic goals, only unrealistic time frames.

Trackable brings us to "The Schwarzenegger Effect." What three words is Arnold best known for in his Terminator films? The three guesses I hear are, "Hasta la vista baby." No, that's four words. "Make my day." Wrong guy, and wrong movie. That of course is Clint Eastwood in *Dirty Harry*. The correct answer is, "I'll be back." The "I'll be back" is what puts teeth into the goal achievement process. What's one thing that every aspiring world class athlete needs? No, it's not the shoes. There you are, an adolescent, a teenager, and you know that you have world class talent. You need a coach. I believe that everybody needs a coach. The only difference between you and a world class athlete is that the athlete knows to go out and get one. A coach will help make sure that your activities are highly relevant. As we discussed before, this is a highly critical piece of the goal achievement process. A coach will help you set up your initial goals, will then look you in the eye and say, "I'll be back." Meaning in one month the two of you will get back together again and review your results. For some people their reaction is, "Great. I'll be able to show them my results and then get the praise, recognition and continued support I need." Being able to tell another person about your successes is a great motivator. I find this to be true of 20 percent of the people I coach. The other 80 percent are thinking, "I better do something. This guy is serious. I don't want to embarrass myself when he does come back." As their coach I really don't care which internal dialogue they're having because either way this approach of people knowing that I'll be back motivates them to take the actions that they have committed to, which will maximize their results. As I said, having a coach who tracks and monitors your progress is what puts teeth into the goal achievement process.

Who is the easiest person to lie to in the world? That is, aside from your mother, father, or your spouse/significant other. Correct—yourself. The role of your coach is to get you to your goal—no matter what! Especially before all the excuses and rationalizing kick in. Notice the word rationalize—there are two ways to write this out. The way you now see it and the way your coach sees it when you start in with all the excuses about why you didn't do what you said you were going to do. Here's the other way to spell rationalize—rational lies. Knowing that the easiest person in the world to lie to is yourself is another important reason why you need a coach—someone who remains objective and knows when you're steering yourself off track, someone who doesn't sympathize at all with your excuses. When we get to the when and the where, the forms of goal setting, we'll discuss these review sessions with your coach in greater depth.

Another point about writing down goals is that they need to be flexible. Just because you have written down a goal doesn't mean that you can't change that goal, or even drop it as a goal. Situations and information changes. So don't be inflexible. Along with goals needing to be S.M.A.R.T; motivational, and challenging, goals also need to be flexible. After we do these next two exercises, I'll give you part two on how to write down goals, part one being goals need to be S.M.A.R.T.

Oh, one other point about the "T." T also stands for technology. Technology to help you track and achieve your goals. Using contact management software to monitor your progress. Having all of your goals, action plans, and coaching tips entered into your computer and programmed to be an additional coach for you.

You have my permission to put all of the forms in this book on your computer.

Getting Ready To Write

We're almost ready to take our first turn at writing down our goals. To help you prime the pump, we're going to go through two exercises that will help us write effectively.

There's an old saying, "When the going gets tough the tough get going." This is certainly true; but another way of looking at it is, "When the going gets tough, the tough go shopping."

Give yourself one minute and see how much money you can spend in one minute. The purpose of this exercise is to help you start thinking about some possible goals. Have fun with this exercise, and don't take it too seriously. Here are the ground rules. First, have the attitude that whatever you write down can be yours—cars, boats, second homes, home/apartment improvements, clothing, whatever material things you can think of that you would like to have. Second, there are two things that you can't write down—an unlimited bank account and the purchase of companies. OK, get ready for your shopping spree. Time your one minute and shop until you drop. "Good morning Kmart shoppers." Go for it.

Now put an estimated dollar amount next to each item that you wrote down, and come up with a grand total. Did you spend over a million dollars? I once gave a seminar to a group of 40 people, and when I asked this million dollar question, all 40 raised their hands. In fact, one of the participants said, "I spent that on shoes alone!"

5 million? 10 million? 50 million? More? Some people spend a couple of thousand; others spend billions. It doesn't really matter. I wanted you to start thinking about some goals that you might want. When we get to the specific categories where I want you to consider setting some goals, I will refer you back to this list that you just generated.

Values

When I saw the movie *Hook*, the story of Peter Pan directed by Steven Spielberg, my glasses must have fogged up a half a dozen times. Especially the scene where Peter, played by Robin Williams, was trying to save a 5 billion dollar development deal. His family kept interrupting him, and finally, at the top of his voice he screamed, "Will everybody just shut up!" His wife had the children leave the room. She then gave Peter some sage advice. She reminded him that his children were at an age when they wanted him to be around, but that this was a very small window of time in number of years. Very quickly they would no longer be interested in his attention. During these precious few years he was missing it. He wasn't being careful.

I fogged up because of how true this scene is for so many of us. It certainly reminded me to treasure my time with my two young daughters. Already the phone and friends were becoming more important than their parents. This scene helped me to be careful of where I was putting my attention, careful that I didn't look back on these years with regret, regret that I hadn't enjoyed and appreciated my family by spending more time with them.

We can get so wrapped up in our pursuit of professional success that we forget why we're working in the first place. Our lives very easily get out of balance. It can lead to an empty "success" story—being professionally successful, but filled with regrets when it comes to any other fulfillment in the other areas of life. The old saying that you'll never hear somebody on his death bed wishing that he had spent more time at the office. Too often the regret is that he spent too little time with his family. Now there is nothing he can do about it. It's just the plain, simple truth that he missed being there as his children grew up, that he didn't make it a high enough priority to make sure that he was there for his family. Yes, you can come up with all the right excuses, but you're still left with the feeling that you blew it.

It comes down to values. What do you value as important in your life? The clearer you are on your values, the clearer you are on what it is that really brings you fulfillment, the more careful you will be on deciding how to spend your time. Your values and your goals need to fit like a hand in a glove. The clearer you are on your values, the clearer and more powerful will be your goals. The goals will be in alignment with those things that really inspire and motivate you towards real success, a success that you can be proud of and at peace with, a success that you created out of your own definition and conviction to what success truly means to you.

I'm going to have you go through a very simple and short value clarification exercise. I emphasize short because you can easily spend hours, perhaps days, focusing in on what your core values/beliefs are. The purpose of this exercise is to give you some initial insights into your values. I certainly recommend that you keep yourself open to the possibility of attending workshops devoted solely to the exploration of values, or perhaps reading a book exclusively devoted to uncovering values. My own experience with this is that even the short time, 10-15 minutes, that we're going to spend on this exercise can give you some excellent insights. Further investigation through workshops and books will help you fine-tune and clarify these initial impressions. The brief time that we're spending on this exercise can effectively move you towards a better understanding of your values.

Turn to the exercise titled **UNDERSTANDING YOUR VALUES** on page 59, and follow the step-by-step instructions.

Pretty interesting stuff isn't it? Now that you have identified your top five values, put them all on one piece of paper. Take an 8 1/2" x 11" piece of paper and, using your PC or colored markers, put the five of them all on this one piece of paper. Place it somewhere in your house or in your office where you'll see your values staring you in the face every day. They'll be a nice reminder to you of what it is that you stand for, what it is that you're willing to live for. Glance at them when you're in your 6 day window, ready to set up your next months goals. More about this six day window when we get to the "when?" of goal setting.

I recommend that you do this value clarification exercise every one to two years. During the New Years period is perfect. Yes, your values do change. As you achieve different goals, as your life situations change, your values are affected—where you need to put your attention, where you choose to put your attention. I first went through this type of exercise in the mid-1980's. Only two of the values in my top five then are still in my top five now. My values seem to be changing less and less over the past few years. Perhaps when I get to my next level of success this will cause a fine-tuning of my values . . . perhaps. I still find it fun to take the 15 minutes to look at my values and to see if anything has changed. As we stated in the exercise directions, there are no right or wrong value answers. It's just that the better you know yourself, the more accurate your answers will be for yourself.

Once you have all five boldly placed on the one piece of paper, ask yourself these three questions: 1) Am I surprised by my #1 value? 2) Am I surprised by any of my top five values? 3) What do these five values or any part of the value clarification exercise tell me about myself and about what goals are the most important to me?

Oh, if you're interested, here are my top five values as of the last time I took this exercise:

1. Personal Development (use of potential)
2. Health (physical and mental well-being)
3. Family Happiness (enjoying sharing your life together)
4. Achievement (accomplishment, mastery, a lasting contribution)
5. Economic Security (freedom from the worry about money)

Understanding Your Values

Read these values.

Achievement (accomplishment, mastery, a lasting contribution)
Ambitious (hardworking, aspiring, self-disciplined)
Adventure (new and challenging experiences; a stimulating, active life)
Capable (competent, effective)
Competitive (winning, taking risks, daring)
Courageous (standing up for your beliefs)
Creative (imaginative, innovative, clever)
Economic Security (freedom from the worry about money)
Fame (being famous, well-known)
Family Happiness (enjoying sharing your life together)
Freedom (independence, self-reliant, self-sufficient, and free choice)
Friendship (close companionship)
Health (physical and mental well-being)
Helpful (working for the welfare of others, improving society)
Inner Harmony (being at peace with oneself)
Integrity (honesty, sincerity, strong character)
Intellectual (intelligent and reflective)
Involvement (working with others, belonging)
Love (affectionate, tender, caring, intimacy)
Loyal (faithful to friends or to a group)
Order (tranquillity, stability, conformity)
Personal Development (use of potential)
Pleasure (fun, laughs, a leisurely lifestyle)
Power (control, authority or influence over others)
Religion (strong religious beliefs, closeness to God)
Responsible (accountable, dependable, reliable)
Self-Respect (pride, sense of personal identity, high self-esteem)
Social Recognition (respect and admiration from others, status)
Wealth (making money, getting rich, prosperity)
Wisdom (a mature understanding of life)

I want you to identify your top five values. There are no right or wrong answers. It's an exercise to help you better understand what's important to you. It will help you to set priorities for your goals.

Step I. Go through all 30 values circling those that are the most important to you. Focus in on the most important. All of these values are important, but circle only those that are the most important to you. Circle at least eight, but no more than ten. This should take 2-3 minutes. Get both your mind and heart involved in your decision. Think about it, and then go with your instincts. The short time doesn't allow for paralysis by analysis.

Step II. Now, from those that you circled, pick out your top five. Put an asterisk next to your top five.

Step III. Rank them #1-5, with #1 being your top value.

When finished ask yourself these four questions:*

1. Am I surprised by my #1 value?
2. Are there any surprises in my top five?
3. What does this exercise tell me about myself?
4. How will these values affect the goals that I set?

I recommend doing this exercise once a year. As goals are achieved, values do change.

Primed

The pump has been primed. You are now ready to start writing down some personal goals. The first set of goals that we wrote down were professional/business goals, those that we wrote on the form entitled, "How I plan to . . . ". Now we need to balance them with our personal goals. Some companies that I have worked with, would tell me to just focus on the business goals and not to bother about personal goals. Recently though, fewer companies have asked me to structure my workshops without at least touching on personal goals. People in business are smarter now. It's all based on two simple questions. "What goes on at home does that affect us at work? What goes on at work does that affect our home life?" The answers are an obvious, "Yes." Nowadays we realize that our personal goals motivate us back on the job. Speaking for myself, at least 2/3 of my personal goals are dependent on how well my business goals are doing. These personal goals definitely motivate me back on the job, since by doing well on the job, I'm positively influencing the accomplishment of most of my personal goals.

---

*The four questions. An obvious influence from my Jewish upbringing.

Oxymoron

A thousand mile journey begins with a single step, and I'm going to give you an oxymoron to make sure that you get started on this goal setting journey towards success. What's the definition of an oxymoron? Give yourself an example of an oxymoron. First the definition: when two words, one right after the other, seemingly contradict one another. The two classics are: jumbo shrimp and military intelligence. Some of my other favorites are: pretty ugly, bitter sweet, sweet sorrow, friendly fire, fresh frozen, country music, small fortune, constructive criticism, peace offensive, good grief and for you cynics out there, good morning. My personal favorite comes out of the health care, insurance industry: death benefits. By the way, the word oxymoron is an oxymoron itself. Oxy means bright, and moron means dull. The oxymoron I'm now asking you to give yourself is **uninterrupted time**.

Five minutes of uninterrupted time. You may never take this opportunity again. Many people will attend a seminar on goal setting or listen to a tape on goals and the seminar leader will tell them that as soon as they get home they need to write down their goals. You have all the best of intentions. Your heart's in the right place, but when you get home you get involved in some special on TV and promise yourself that you're going to set your goals first thing the next morning. Now it's morning and you're running a little behind, so you need to push off the goals to a bit later in the day. Then each day has its own little excuse and before you know it, nine months have gone by, and you haven't set a single goal down on paper, much less even thought about and come up with a specific goal to carry around in your head. At one of my workshops a participant told me, "Mark, I have a goal. My goal is that by this Friday I have a goal." Hey, it's a start.

I implore you to **just do it**! Remember, studies show that only 1-5 percent of people actually do have written goals. Join and stay in with the **few who do**. OK, let's help you get focused. Let's keep this writing down of goals nice and simple. I'm going to give you twelve categories with some space for writing down your goals.

Here are the ground rules. First of all, I'm not saying that to have balance in your life you need to have three goals in each of the twelve categories. The category headings are there just to help you with some suggestions on where you might want to consider setting some goals. Look at the category heading, and if something comes to mind write it down; if not, move on to the next category and come back to this blank category later. You might have ten goals in one category, or you might have none. It's your decision. Second ground rule. I want you to approach these categories like a child working with a Christmas list. A child has no problem coming up with page after page of very specific gifts he wants. Give this same list to an adult, and he's hard pressed to come up with two or three gifts that really turn him on. Work with this list in a state of childlike innocence. Brainstorming rules are in effect again. Turn off that critical side of your mind, and go for quantity of goals. Don't be concerned with whether these goals are attainable and realistic at this point. Just go for it, or as Jim Carrey would say, "Smokin'." Keep that pen moving. Get it smokin'.

Here are the twelve categories, with a little commentary on each, so you know a bit more about the category to help you with your focus. I want to help get you into the flow, into a zone of heightened awareness and excitement. Like a child.

Family Goals

The extended family—goals concerning a spouse, daughter, son, parent, brother, sister, grandparent, aunt, uncle, cousin, in-laws. For example: spend more (with more being *very* specific) time with spouse, or spend less time with spouse, or find a spouse.

Health and Fitness

These goals are nice and easy to get specific. Exercise, weight, nutrition, learning relaxation techniques goals.

Personal Development

Books, seminars, continuing education, audio and video cassettes. Examples: I read a book on sales every month. I attend a seminar once a quarter. Call this number: **1-800-525-9000.** When you call, someone on the other end of the line will say, "Good morning/afternoon, Nightingale-Conant." Nightingale-Conant is the largest distributor in the world of audio and videocassette programs. Ask him to put you on the mailing list and to send you their free catalog. You will receive a catalog of about 80 pages of the finest speakers in the world. Well, that is except one. But that is a written goal of mine—to have N-C carry my programs. They have a 30 day free trial period on all of their programs. They're really a class act. They'll never hassle you. Being on their mailing list will keep you informed of the latest releases.

I got into audiocassette listening years ago. Without a doubt it has had a tremendously positive impact on my learning. Do you do a lot of driving? Driving is the perfect time to listen to an educational/motivational tape. I have over a hundred programs in my cars trunk. Some people say that they don't even know if their car radio works any more because a tape is always going. My recommendation is to make listening to audiocassettes a habit. Listen to at least one side of one tape whenever you're in your car, or whenever you have the opportunity to listen to tapes, such as when you're exercising. Make listening to audiocassettes a goal.

Travel Goals

You can have some great fun here. My wife, Terry, and I have literally decided on 62 different places that we want to travel to. For me it's by the age of 62, for Terry it's by next summer. I put all 62 places on one piece of paper, and then surrounded them with pictures of these wonderful vacation spots. This technique is called poster boarding. Every time I see a picture of one of these places in a magazine, in a piece of mail, I just cut it out and tape it around this paper. As I walk into my office, I see all of these exotic places I'm going to visit. I love looking at these pictures, but I'll love it even more when I get there; and get there I will. In the meantime, I'm enjoying the beautiful and colorful pictures that remind me of where I'm going, and soon. When we get to the "Where?" of goal setting, I'm going to suggest a form to use to start writing down goals that generate a lot of them.

Community Goals

What organizations do you want to get involved in? more involved in? less involved in? What capacity will be your involvement?

Material Goals

Back to your "shopping spree" exercise where we wanted to see how much money you could spend in one minute. Now I want you to review this list, and then write down in this category's section which of these material goals you're really serious about and are willing to write down as a goal. I recommend at least writing down goals that concern a car, a home, home or apartment improvements and clothing. Of course, don't stop here. But these are three areas that I recommend as excellent areas to start.

Financial Goals

Remember the study highlighting that the 3 percent who had clear written goals with action plans that they implemented had a financial net worth more than the other 97 percent combined? Well, it is now your turn to officially join this upper 3 percent. It is my job to then give you a complete system, which you are now getting, not only to join this upper 3 percent, but to stay in this upper 3 percent for the rest of your life. In this section, I recommend that at the very least, during your five minutes of initial goal setting, you write down your income goals for the next two years. I say at least because at this stage you may not be clear enough about where you want your income goals to be in three, five, ten, and twenty years from now. But you can certainly take a good shot at setting some initial two year income targets. Of course, if you came to this book and to this section already a professional, disciplined, habitual goal setter in the financial realm, here are some guidelines on how to really go for it. Those of you who are just starting to flex your goal setting muscles, this setting of your next two years' income goals is a great place to start.

On the average the 3 percenters from the study had in 1953 set one, two, three, five, ten, and twenty year income goals. They also had short, intermediate and long term savings and investment goals. They also had set a time frame for retirement, with a specific nest egg dollar amount as a goal, so that they would remain financially independent—free from the worry about money throughout their retirement years. So for you sophisticated, dedicated goal achievers, start setting these types of financial, savings, investments and retirement goals when you get to this section. For those of you at the beginning stages, start with your two year goals, and over time you will develop a clearer and clearer vision of what you want your financial goals to be with regards to savings, investments and retirement.

Productivity Goals

You already started working on this section when you did the exercise, **How I plan to increase/impact productivity . . . Where I need to set goals**. If you think you got everything down that you needed to get down for this section during that exercise, you certainly may skip this section. This five minute period gives you a second chance to add as necessary.

Career Goals

Promotion goals. Where do you see yourself with your company in one, three, five, ten years from now? If you want to be president of your company in ten years, what are the positions you would need to be in before becoming the president? Use the technique of beginning with the end in mind and then working your way back to your current position. Write down these positions, with their corresponding time frames. Do you have goals concerning working for another company in a position that better suits, challenges you? Do you aspire to someday own your own company? What are your goals/vision for this company?

Emotional Goals

Yes, for some of these you can still get them very specific. Goals such as "I am assertive." "I am patient." "I am a better listener." "I am a kind and loving person." A good technique to help you get these goals specific is to think, "When I am an assertive person, what will I see myself doing that I'm not now doing?" Then make a list of these activities and share them with your coach for additional feedback on what to add or delete.

But, if you're struggling with getting an emotional goal specific, not to worry. I do believe in writing down affirmations. An affirmation is where you affirm to yourself what it is that you want to become. We know the power of writing something down, so we definitely want to take advantage of this power even though we may not be all that specific on these type of goals. Affirming, "I am patient." "I am a loving and kind person." "I am at peace with myself." "I have high self esteem." "I respect other people." Writing it down will keep this value top of mind for you. Over time you will develop this quality, and the affirmation will become clearer and clearer to you, on what it means to be that kind of person. The affirmation becomes more and more specific, becomes a reality in your life.

Here are three of my favorite affirmations, "I advance confidently in the direction of my dreams." "I act as though it were impossible to fail." "Life is good and the best is yet to come." I have been affirming these three for years, and they have definitely become a part of who I am. I think them almost every morning, quietly repeating them in my mind several times, while taking a shower. Develop your own personal and powerful affirmations.

Social Goals

Goals that concern friends, hobbies or social events. As you know I believe very strongly in having balance in your life. I meet too many people who are not enjoying their success. They're so wrapped up in their business that they start to burn out, they stop having fun.

This happened to me when I first started my business. I was so absorbed in my business that I wasn't making time, or even thinking about time with my friends. Fortunately for me I caught this lack of balance in my life in time. Having great friends is an important value in my life, and I suddenly realized that none of my friends were calling me any more. I guess I was becoming a bore. Part of the problem was that I wasn't calling them. So, I literally set a goal to start calling my friends again. I wrote out a short but important list of people who I definitely wanted to keep in my life. Keeping my commitment to this goal certainly saved several valuable friendships for me. If you need to, set some goals that revolve around friends.

Set social goals. For Terry and me it's setting specific goals for the number of times in a year that we go to Broadway plays, classical music events, and museums. For us this is the icing on the cake of success, an important part of "the good life" for us.

Don't go to your grave with your wonderful hobbies never being developed. Hobbies are an effective and passionate way to manage stress. An effective way to bring out your full potential. Just by writing goals down in these three areas of friends, social events, and hobbies will keep them top of mind, and motivate you to take action. Remember, there are two pains in life, the pain of discipline, or the pain of regret. Which one will you choose?

Spiritual Goals

Private, family, and/or congregational. I think these three say it all.

Prime Time

It's now time for you to join the upper 1-5 percent, those who have taken the time to write out their goals.

Time at least five minutes. You may need more to get most of the goals that you want to get down in these twelve categories. You'll be amazed by how much you can accomplish in five minutes. In my workshops, this is the amount of time that I give the seminar participants. For most of the people five minutes is more than enough. But this is just a general guideline. For some people two minutes is enough. For others you may need a half an hour or more. Perhaps you need to go off on a personal retreat and immerse yourself in solitude for several days. Everybody is different. But I am amazed at how much can be accomplished in such a short period of time. So, at the very least, give yourself the gift of five minutes of uninterrupted time. Find a place where you will not be disturbed.

I'm not saying that you need to have three goals in each of these twelve categories to create balance in your life. The twelve categories are there just to help you with your focus. You certainly may not have goals in all these areas, or you may have created more than the twelve I have suggested. The three bullets are there just to create some space for you to write in. You may have no goals in one area, or you may have a dozen. As always, it's your call. Approach this like a child with a Christmas list. Be innocent, and keep that pen moving.

If you wish, use the format supplied on the next couple of pages, or create your own format. The important thing is to do it, and do it now! Go for it!

AN INVENTORY OF YOUR GOALS, YOUR DREAMS

Note: A dream is a goal with wings.

1. **Family Goals**

   -
   -
   -

2. **Health and Fitness Goals**

   -
   -
   -

3. **Personal Development Goals**

-
-
-

4. **Travel Goals**

-
-
-

5. **Community Goals**

-
-
-

6. **Material Goals**

-
-
-

7. **Financial Goals**

-
-
-

8. **Productivity Goals**

-
-
-

9. **Career Goals**

-
-
-

10. **Emotional Goals**

-
-
-

11. **Social Goals**

-
-
-

12. **Spiritual Goals**

-
-
-

CONGRATULATIONS!!!

In all sincerity, congratulations. What you just did, only one to five percent of the people in our world will ever take the time to do.

You have now joined the upper 1-5 percent, now let me give you some additional information to help keep you in this upper echelon.

Step IV: How To . . . Part Deux . . . The Three P's

The first part of how to set goals is that goals need to be S.M.A.R.T, challenging and flexible. Part two of how to set goals has to do with the three P's.

Review the pages where you wrote down your goals. The page titled **"How I Plan to Increase/Impact Productivity"** and the pages of goals that you just wrote. Pick out the five goals that you want to achieve more than any others. Any five. It can be more than one goal from any category. It can be a mix of personal and professional. It can be all business or all personal. Now, circle the five that turn you on the most. Those that really get the fire in your belly, the fire in your heart burning.

OK. We're going to use these five to practice how to use the three P's in a moment. To me, a goal statement is a simple one or two liner. What I am about to tell you about how to write down a goal is not the only way to write down goals, but it certainly is a very simple way. Here are the three P's:

- ◆ **Personal**—Write your goal in the personal. A goal has to be your own, something that you want and believe you can accomplish. A goal can certainly be influenced by others, but the final decision to truly make a commitment to it, to have a strong desire to achieve it, comes from you. Writing goals in the personal means somewhere in the goal statement use the word I, Me, My, Our, We . . .

- ◆ **Positive**—Write down what you want rather than what you want to avoid. For example, if you're a golfer, you wouldn't write down, "I never slice my shot." You would write down, "I hit the fairway 65 percent of the time." Another example. Instead of "I'm never late," I recommend, "I show up on time. I'm 5-10 minutes early for 90 percent of my appointments and right on time for the other 10 percent."

- ◆ **Present Tense**—Write the goal down as if it is already true, as if it has already happened. Not, "I will earn $100,000.00," but "I earn $100,000.00." One of my seminar participants said that he had learned to write goals down in the past tense, meaning, "I earned $100,000.00 in 1996." He said that this made it more of a done deal. As I said, what I'm teaching you is not the only way, so you decide for yourself what best suits you. The purpose of writing it in the present tense is that it drives the message home to you simply and powerfully.

Another seminar participant of mine once asked, "Do you write down I am married when you're still single?" Oh well, there's that flexibility I mentioned. In this case it makes sense to write down, "I will be married by . . . " then putting in a dateline for you to shoot for. Or, you could leave it, "I am married," as an affirmation of a value that is important to you. When it comes to the best way to write down a goal, I recommend that you don't over intellectualize and obsess over whether you wrote it down correctly or not . . . the more important factor is just doing it, and getting your desired results.

Here are two other points on how to write goals before I have you practice on your five. When I'm working with people on their goals, too often I see people writing down, "I will try . . . " I recommend that you don't use the word try. Just drop it from your habit of writing down goals. Too often "try" represents, "I really don't believe I can do it, but I'll try." As the great master Yoda taught Luke Skywalker, "**Do or do not, there is no try.**" Great advice. And to simplify your goals, I also recommend dropping the word "will." Now, for some people the word "will" greatly inspires them, so leave it in if you wish.

Here are some examples of goal statements using both the S.M.A.R.T and the three P's of goal setting. Write down both the mission and the how to goals as appropriate:

"I earn $100,000.00 in 1996."
  —*I work with ten new clients in 1996.*

"I weigh 165 pounds by June 22, 1996."
  —*I start a three times a week exercise program by March 1.*

"I drive a 1996 Lexus LS 400. I lease it in July, 1996."

"I make 30 prospecting phone calls a day."
  —*I prioritize my account list into A, B, C prospects by the end of the first quarter.*

"I have 10 appointments a week."

"My proposal to ABC Corp is accepted in May, 1996."
  Note: *These last three goals will help me achieve my first goal, the income goal.*

Now, in the space provided, write down the five goals you picked as your most important goals, as personal, positive, present tense goal statements. Make these goals S.M.A.R.T.

-

-

-

-

-

P.S. This picking out of your five most important goals and then writing them down to practice how to write goals is Step 4 in our 5 step goal achievement process. The first three being, 1) Desire, 2) Belief, and 3) Write it down.

The When and the Where of Goal Setting
When?

I promised you a K.I.S.S. throughout this whole process. Here is where I continue to deliver on this promise. I know that even if everything we've discussed makes sense to you intellectually and that you know in your heart and in your gut that this goal setting process will be of great benefit to you, but it's hard to do . . . you probably won't do it. So if you remember nothing else that we've discussed and do nothing else but this one thing, you will benefit from this system.

Set goals on a monthly basis. Once a month, take 15-30 minutes to write down your goals for the upcoming month. I recommend a month based on my experience of coaching thousands of people through this system. A month seems to work for most people, whether you're a novice, someone who has never written down a goal in your life, or whether you're a dedicated, disciplined, habitual goal setter.

For me to ask someone who has never written down a goal to write down their six month, one year, five, ten, and twenty year goals is next to impossible. The frustration will be too great. The goals will probably be too meaningless and the goal achievement process will be quickly abandoned. "This stuff is too hard, too frustrating, why bother?" will be the predicted reaction.

But even for people who have never written down a goal, I have found that a month is something they can wrap their mind around. Using the system from this book, doing and following the step-by-step that I have provided, will give them the necessary momentum to easily get started. I recommend getting started with a month.

Give yourself a six day window in which to write down your upcoming months goals. For example, if you're about to set up your June goals, anywhere from May 29-June 3 you would take the 15-30 minutes to write down your June goals. I say 15-30 minutes based on my experience of doing this myself for over a decade, plus by asking my clients how long it takes them to write down their monthly goals.

My monthly calendar, daily priority lists and the previous months goals all influence the setting up of the upcoming months goals. For example, the first thing I look at to set my new goals is my previous months goals. This accomplishes two things: 1) it forces me to track my results, and 2) I get to see which goals I need to carry over into the next month. Let's now look at these two a little more deeply.

Tracking results is part of setting S.M.A.R.T. goals and part of **"The Schwarzenegger/General MacArthur Effect."** The "I'll be back," the "I shall return," piece of the goal achievement process to help you maximize your results. T = Trackable and is ideally accomplished with your coach. You may choose to meet with your coach every month or at least once a quarter. The months that you don't meet face-to-face or discuss your goals over the phone, send, fax, or e-mail your coach your goals to keep them updated on your current focus and commitments. Remember from our discussion of the role, the power of having a coach is that it motivates you to take action. It disciplines you to keep your promises and commitments to yourself. It motivates you to "look good" in your coach's eyes. It motivates you to get the praise, recognition, support and encouragement we all love to get. Knowing that you're going to meet with your coach also motivates you by triggering, in a positive way, the fear of failure, the fear of criticism. Knowing that a meeting is coming up during your six day window with your coach will motivate you to take action, since you certainly don't want to look foolish or inept to your coach. Foolish in the sense that you haven't made significant progress towards your goals or that you come across as mediocre. These monthly coaching meetings can be held in your office, or you may want to meet over a meal, away from the office.

In tracking your results, I recommend using a simple yes, no, abstention system and then figuring out what percent of your goals you hit for that month. I simply review each of my previous months goals by myself or with my coach and put a Y, N, or A next to each one. Sometimes the Y is a percentage. My goal was to earn $10,000.00 that month and my actual came in at $9,000.00. I'll put 90 percent next to that goal. Some other goals are a straight-forward Y or N, but some may fall into the A category. For instance, my goal was to set up an appointment or to get a commitment from someone, and for reasons beyond my control, the decision was tabled for the upcoming month or several months in the future. So put an A next to the goal.

If the goal is still an important goal, I'll simply write it down in the appropriate month. Important goal meaning that things do change, remembering that goals need to be flexible. Situations and circumstances do change, and this changing information definitely influences your commitments, where you decide to focus your attention. No longer important? No longer a goal or a differently worded goal.

Here's a rule of thumb for whether to write down a goal or not. I suggest that you keep writing something down as long as by writing it down, it keeps this goal at the top of your mind and will motivate you to take action. As we'll discuss in the time management section, what gets written gets done. But once something is a habit, meaning whether you write it down or not, it will be done. You don't need to write it down any longer since it's no longer a goal, but a done deal. For example, you have decided that exercising three times a week is a very important goal for you. Keep on writing it down as a goal until it becomes a regular routine for you. But as long as there might still be some doubt whether you'll do it or not, or that you might backslide, keep on writing it down, month after month.

Once I have assigned a Y, a percentage, a N or an A, I'll then come up with a percentage for what amount of goals I hit in that month. Ten goals with 6 Y's, one N, 2 A's, and a 90 percentile will track at 75 percent (six out of seven, with the 90 percent moving my overall average up) of my goals being hit, and I'll write this percentage in the upper right hand corner of my goal form. More about this goal form and how it can be used as a journal in our next section.

Reviewing my previous months goals is the first step in setting up the next months goals. Then I'll look at my upcoming month's calendar, and set specific goals around these upcoming appointments and workshops. I write them down, being S.M.A.R.T, and use the three P's. Then I'll look through my 1-31's, my upcoming daily priority lists either written in my planner or entered into my contact management software, to find more goals that I need to keep top of mind. More about this daily priority list in the time management section. These three steps in 15-30 minutes.

Another guideline. Let's say that you are expecting commitments from quite a few prospects, clients, in one month. Instead of writing out a one-two line goal for each one, you can write it out this way, "I get "Yes" commitments from . . . " and then list out each of the names as one goal statement. You certainly can write out a one line goal for each if you feel that this will better highlight each goal for you. No cookie cutter approaches. Whatever works best for you.

Where?

There are four forms to be used in the goal achievement process.

- A one-part monthly form
- A four-part form for intermediate (months 2-5) goals
- A tri-fold for long term (6 months and out) goals
- A form for "possibility/dream" goals

Please refer to each of the four formats provided in this book.

The One-Part

Use this for your monthly goal setting. The international sign for "no whining" is on the monthly form to remind you to just do it. I guarantee that certain months during your six day window, the whiner within all of us will peek its ugly head out. The whining associated with goal setting usually goes something like this, "I don't have the time." "This won't work for me." "I don't want to do this. It's too hard. I don't hit all of my goals, why bother?" The sign is there to remind you that it is normal to have these thoughts. We all do. Just ignore these thoughts, and then just write down your goals. Even after all of these years of goal setting, I still get this quiet little voice running around in my head. I'm not surprised by it, and I'm certainly not thrown off course by it. While it's whispering in my ear, I'm innocently writing down my goals.

The monthly form is also incorporated into the four-part so people won't be calling me and whining, "Mark, I lost my form. I haven't set any goals." Here's a goal for you. Within 24 hours of reading this, take this four-part to a copier and make 15 copies so that you'll have a five-year, 60-month supply. Also make 12 copies of the one-part monthly form for a full years supply.

76 Part II • The Power of Goals

My Monthly Goals

For the month of _____

~~Whining~~

Personal Goals
_____

Family Goals
_____

Business Goals
_____
_____
_____
_____
_____
_____
_____
_____
_____
_____
_____
_____
_____
_____

© 1999 Human Resources Unlimited

This is for your monthly goal setting. During your end-of-month 6 day window, look at your previous month's goals to determine what goals need to be carried to the next month. Then look at your upcoming month's calendar to see what goals are in these commitments and appointments. Then look at your Daily Priority Lists (1-31's) for goals.

This will take you 15-30 minutes once a month. A small investment leading to huge results.

When completed, cut it out and put it into the tri-fold to carry around. This way you can look at your goals throughout the month. (Additional forms at back of book.)

As a general rule of thumb expect to have 1-2 personal goals, 1-2 family goals and anywhere from 4-9 business goals. But like most rules, these are made to be broken. Some months you'll have more or less. It doesn't matter. Now, you may be thinking, "Hey Mark, where's the balance? Too many business goals compared to personal and family." Not to worry. The "possibility/dream" form will get us the balance we're looking for.

But before we discuss that form, let's look at a second form called the four-part.

The Four-Part

Ever have this experience? You're sitting at a red light and all of a sudden this great idea/goal comes washing over you in all its glory. You clearly see its attainment, all the steps involved, you're filled with great excitement and enthusiasm. The light then turns green; you make a left, a right; someone honks a horn, and whoosh, the idea's gone or left half-baked. As we know from Yul Brynner, "So, let it be written. So, let it be done."

Use this four-part form for writing down your intermediate goals, goals for months two through five. This way you'll remember them. When you're in your six day window, you'll already have several goals written down. This is why a lot of people keep paper/a hand held recorder in their car's glove compartment or paper and pen by their nightstand to capture these flashes of brilliance.

Long term planning used to be five, ten, twenty year plans. With the world changing so rapidly and information pouring into us from so many sources, I find it more practical and workable to define one month as short term, two to five months as intermediate, and anything six months and out as long term.

The Tri-Fold

This form is to be used for your long term goals. **Note:** This form may be blank for several months or for several years. For myself, I had no goals beyond the month for over five years. When I first started getting into goal setting, I was one of those people who was fooling myself into believing that I was a goal setter. You know, one of those who had goals but didn't need to write them down. I believed in goal setting, knew most of the reasons why I should be setting goals, but in reality had totally deluded myself into thinking I was a focused, dedicated goal setter. Not! Fortunately for my-

My Monthly Goals
For the month of _____ **Whining** 🚫

Personal Goals

Family Goals

Business Goals

© 1999 Human Resources Unlimited

My Monthly Goals
For the month of _____ **Whining** 🚫

Personal Goals

Family Goals

Business Goals

© 1999 Human Resources Unlimited

My Monthly Goals
For the month of _____ **Whining** 🚫

Personal Goals

Family Goals

Business Goals

© 1999 Human Resources Unlimited

My Monthly Goals
For the month of _____ **Whining** 🚫

Personal Goals

Family Goals

Business Goals

© 1999 Human Resources Unlimited

Four-Part Monthly Form

self, I realized that I was deluding myself, and finally made a conscious decision to make a commitment to goal setting.

So, I just put my head down, didn't listen to all those voices telling me not to bother with this goal setting stuff, and every month, religiously, I would set my monthly goals.

It is true that the toughest step to take in a thousand mile journey is the first step. It didn't matter, I just took what I thought were some good first steps. I looked for a coach but didn't find any that would stick with me. I made some progress. I even had some goals beyond the month, but nothing really crystal clear. Some vision of where I was headed, but nothing truly definitive. Then it happened. I hit my critical mass. Enough months and years of goal setting, and goal achievement finally started to give me a clearer vision of where I wanted to take my business and my life. It happened after almost five years of goal setting. Until that time, my four-part and my tri-fold for intermediate and long term goals was completely blank. Now I have enough goals on that form that I probably need to live to be 189 years old to get to half of these goals. Goals that are ten years, twenty years and beyond, that are very specific and meaningful. It's exciting. It's a great feeling. Finally to be able to answer my third grade teachers question of, "What do you want to be when you grow up?"

So, if you come to this goal achievement process well versed and well oiled in the power of goal setting, you might be in a position to use this form immediately. For some of you, perhaps a couple of months of goal setting will give you a clearer vision of where you're heading. Put these longer term goals on the tri-fold. For others, like myself, it may take a bit longer. All you need to do is take care of the present months goals, and the future goals will start to unfold at their own pace. The message is simple. Take care of your month to month goals, and the future will unfold for you. Again, back to the wisdom of getting some initial instruction and then just doing it!

The Possibilities/Dream Form

This is the form where you can write out all of your personal and family goals to your hearts delight. This is where you can get that balance between personal and professional development goals.

I told you that Terry, my wife, and I had written down 62 places that we wanted to travel to. Before putting them all down on one piece of paper, I had used the form, **What I Want to Accomplish During My Life**, which you'll find on page 82.

Part II • The Power of Goals

My Goals

Personal Goals
_____
_____
_____

Family Goals
_____
_____
_____
_____

Business Goals
_____
_____
_____
_____
_____
_____
_____
_____
_____
_____
_____
_____
_____

© 1999 Human Resources Unlimited

Use this tri-fold for your long term goals. Additional forms available at the back of the book.

I first heard about this technique in a story someone told me about Lou Holtz, the great Notre Dame football coach. It seems that Lou, when he was a young assistant football coach, had been fired. He was upset about this when a friend gave him some good advice. He told Lou to take a blank piece of paper, title the paper, **What I Want to Accomplish During My Life**, and to write down as many things as came to his mind. He wrote down 108 things. Over the years he has accomplished over 80 of them and is constantly adding to his list. A great exercise.

I suggest that you keep a similar **"possibilities"** list for yourself. I have written down over 50 possibility goals for myself. Possibility, meaning it's an idea/goal that is intriguing, but one that I'm not ready or prepared to get S.M.A.R.T. For me it's the possibility of writing some books, tentative titles for them, audio and video training programs, how large I want to grow my business, my vision of how my business might make a difference in this world, things of this nature.

I keep this form in a drawer in my office, and whenever some idea(s) starts to bubble up (but I'm not too sure of where it may lead me or how serious I am about taking action on it), I'll just store it on this sheet. It's important to write these possibilities down because you never know when you might really want to take action on it. Then, because you haven't written it down, you can't even remember what it was. All you remember is that you had some good idea that left a good feeling with you, got you excited, and now you can't retrieve it.

Also, it's fun every once in a while to look at this list and see what you wrote down. It might take you nowhere, or it might prove to be the foundation for some inspiring ideas and goals.

Ever have a really great idea, one that fills you up with a lot of excitement? This idea is so powerful, such an obviously simple idea that you think to yourself, "I don't need to write this one down. No way am I going to forget this idea." Five minutes later, you have no clue of what that idea was. It's lost for the moment, or forever. If it's that important it will probably come back around. But why leave it to chance? Don't think it ink it. Just take a nanosecond to write it down.

Carry, Look and Work

Here are some additional tips on how to maximize on the power of these written goals on these forms.

The Possibilities/Dream Form

Dream to your heart's content. Let your imagination run wild.

What I Want to Accomplish During My Life

-
-
-
-
-
-

NOTE: Make up your own additional sheets. The sky's the limit!

Carry

I work with a lot of advertising sales teams. I learned that one of the most important advertising principles is that of **frequency**. The more times that you see an advertisement, the deeper is driven the message and its influence. I want you to think of your written goals as your advertisement to yourself. The more frequently you look at your goals, the more powerful their message to you and your commitment to them.

Take your upcoming months' goals, put them on a smaller four-part monthly format, fold them down and **carry** them on your person. I suggest that you look at them at least three times a week, if not three times a day. It's your call. Be natural about it. Whenever you feel the urge to glance at your goals, just read through them. This will remind you of your commitments and it will remind you if you have planned or are clear on your next steps. Whenever I read through my goals, I simply use this as an opportunity for me to check in on myself, to make sure that I'm clear on what my next steps are. This is all part of the action planning of goal achievement.

Look

Take your monthly goal sheet, and enlarge it to 11" x 17". A nice big sheet that you can't miss. Or, take your 8 1/2" x 11" monthly sheet and post it/tape it where you can see it. The first thing that you see as you enter my office is my enlarged goal sheet right across from my desk, staring me right in the face. In-your-face goals. No way I'm going to forget my commitments! Staring you right in the face, not only in your workplace, but how about at home? Stick a magnet on it, and there they are on your refrigerator. Let your imagination run wild with the possibilities of how often you'll see your goals, coming in all shapes and sizes.

Work

Have a blank four-part form posted on your work desk or in a drawer that you open frequently, or anyplace that is conspicuous and easily accessible. Write in the months for the next four months in their proper space. The purpose of this is to make it as easy as possible for you when you're in your six day window for setting up the next month's goals. For example, it's January 2 and you've just finished writing down your January goals. A blank four-part is taped on your desk for the months February through May. Whenever an idea/an inspiration for a goal in any of these months comes up, write it down in the appropriate month. If the idea is specifically for a goal out six months or more, write it on your long term tri-fold form. If it's a "just a feeling goal," place it on your possibility form. This way, when you're in your six day window, you may have several goals already written down, and you'll be well on your way to quickly finalizing these upcoming months' goals. This is just a suggestion. You might post the four-part, and never write anything down on it. In this case, just set the upcoming months goals using all the recommendations I have outlined to facilitate the setting of monthly goals.

Save Your Goals as a Journal

After you have reviewed the results of your previous month and assigned a percent of accomplishment to it, **don't throw away the monthly form**. Save it. Over the years these forms can serve as a very interesting journal/diary. A journal of where you've been and where you're going. It's fun to look back and see all the progress you've made. Hey, some day you may write down a goal to write a book or produce something where this type of journal will prove to be invaluable to you. Keep it in written form, saved in your computer, on a disk or all three.

This journal will help you better appreciate all that you have accomplished. It minimizes the, "What have I done with my life?" question, the one that doesn't come up with any satisfactory answers.

This journal, by tracking your accomplishments, does wonders for your self-esteem.

Visualization

People are always asking me about visualization. Obviously I'm a believer. I have already mentioned the fun and power of poster boarding your vacation/travel goals. The door frame to my office is surrounded by beautiful pictures, from magazines, postcards, direct mail pieces, of all the places I dream to visit with my family, with Terry, or just by myself.

As Norman Vincent Peale explained it: Verbalize, Visualize, Emotionalize, and Realize.

There's no world class athlete who doesn't visualize his success first in his mind, before realizing it on the field of competition. Visualization can be a very powerful technique to help you realize more of your goals. You can use this very simple format to help you get started.

Write down the most important goal you are now working on:

Visualization

Write a detailed description of the positive sensory impressions you will experience when your goal is achieved:

Sight:

Sound:

Touch:

Taste:

Smell:

Emotion/What You Will Feel:

What will you see when you accomplish your goal? What will you hear, touch, taste, smell and feel when your goal is realized?

Chapter Seven

It Starts and Ends with Desire

Step V: Determination and Persistence

The story goes that when Winston Churchill was in his eighties and retired, he was invited by his prep school to address the young men about the greatest lessons he had learned during his life. His talk was six words.

The elderly gentleman got up out of his seat, slowly walked to the podium, leaned forward on his cane, and said, "Never give up. Never, never, never."

Great advice, great wisdom. As we learned several chapters back, a large part of success is not giving up. Simply stated, your determination and persistence measure your belief in yourself!

What do most people do regarding the goal achievement process? That's right, they give up. They might read this book, attend a seminar, listen to an audio, watch a video on goal setting. They get all excited . . . that is, for two or three days. Then right back to their old habits of being and staying unfocused, of not setting goals.

This cartoon perfectly captures the state of our world concerning learning something, and then **not** using it, perfectly captures the truth that knowledge is *potential* power. This cartoon also reminds me of the Robert Frost poem, *The Road Less Traveled*. The lines where he describes a fork in the road, and says that he took the road less traveled. Taking this road made all the difference in his life. Making goal setting a habit can make a difference in your life.

In the cartoon, there is a fork in the road with a huge arrow above the crossing, pointing for people to follow the road to the right. Where's everybody, or at least 95-99 percent of the people going? To the left. Why? Because that's where everybody else is going. Following the followers. If you're going to follow someone, make sure you're following a leader. Be the few who do! Set and achieve goals, and get a coach to help keep you on the road less traveled.

◆ **GOAL #1 START! Begin the process, the journey**

—Well begun is half done. Beware of the **law of diminishing intent** which states that the best time to start anything new is before the initial enthusiasm and emotion have passed. The longer you wait to get started, the slimmer the chances are that you will get started. I once heard it said that character and integrity is doing what you say you're going to do.

◆ **GOAL #2 CONTINUE!**

—Give it at least six months. Make goal setting and goal achievement a new habit. More about this when we discuss the goal achievement curve.

- ◆ **GOAL #3   RESULTS!**
    —I guarantee it. Over a very short period of time, by dedicating yourself to just setting down your monthly goals, your goals will get more and more specific and meaningful. The results will be there for you. Everybody moves at his own pace, but the results will be there. Never give up. Never, never, never.

- ◆ **GOAL #4   PEACE of MIND, INNER CONTENTMENT, HAPPINESS**
    —The goal of all goals. Why we do what we do.

The Goal Achievement Curve

This curve helps drive home the point, once again, that a large part of your success is not giving up. Look at the goal achievement curve. Think of the beginning of the curve, the far left, as where you are today with regards to your commitment to goal setting.

Whenever you start something new, the effort and energy that you have to put into it is high, while your results and effectiveness are low. This partially explains the "first step is the toughest step" experience.

This curve also explains very accurately that **everything is a process**. As you move along the curve, what happens over time is that the effort and energy becomes less and less, while your results and effectiveness start to improve. Eventually the two lines cross, and this is the crossover to "working smarter, not harder," and "doing less, but accomplishing more." Unfortunately, where do most people stop? That's right, either right at the one yard line, which is just before the lines cross, or well before they have even come close to giving goal setting a chance. Thomas Edison's quote right under the curve says it all.

Why do people quit so close to success? In addition to what we've discussed in, "why don't people set goals?" I think there is one other fear we haven't touched on . . . the fear of success. Fear of success? Why would anyone be afraid of success? Not being a psychologist, I won't get too deep into this, but here's some information I've read on this subject.

Two things come to mind. One, that we get mixed messages about the pursuit of success, the pursuit of money. "Money is the root of all evil." "Make as much as you can." "Rich people are thieves." "You can't be wealthy and honest at the same time." "Money is a measure, a yardstick, of your success." So we're left with a lot of ambivalence concerning achieving success. This ambivalence can lead to you sabotag-

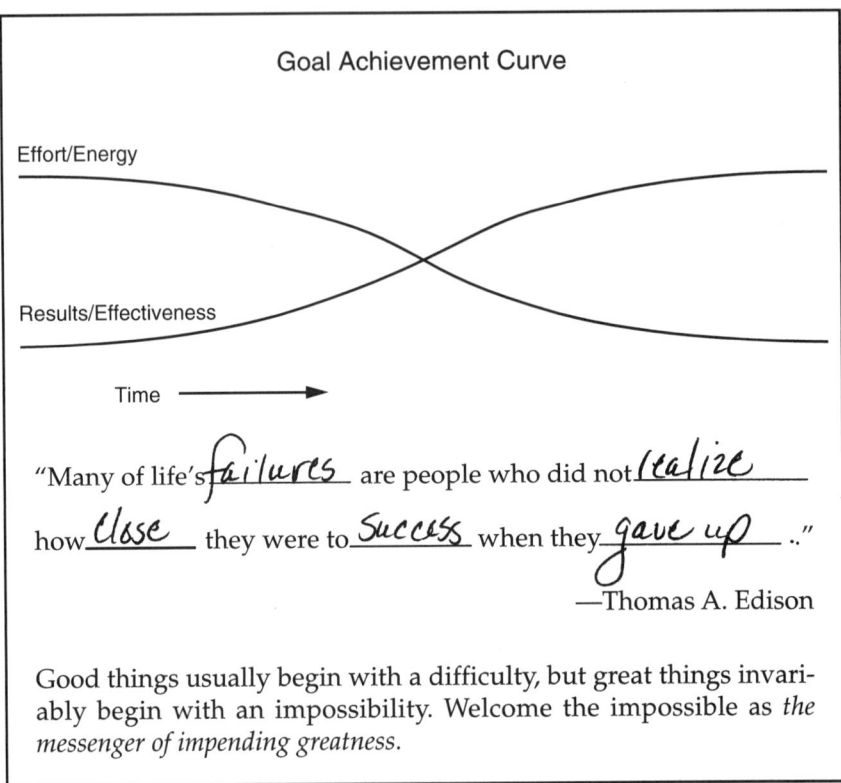

"Many of life's _failures_ are people who did not _realize_ how _close_ they were to _success_ when they _gave up_.."

—Thomas A. Edison

Good things usually begin with a difficulty, but great things invariably begin with an impossibility. Welcome the impossible as *the messenger of impending greatness.*

ing your success right at the one yard line, just before you create some exciting results and accomplishments in your life. Sabotaging, like quitting on simple, effective habits such as goal setting.

The second reason why people fear success, is that they're afraid that people won't like them any more. You know that old worn out mantra, "It's lonely at the top". Nonsense. Of course it can be lonely at the top, but it can also get very lonely at the bottom as well. This loneliness at the top is more a factor of who you are and the balance you create, or don't create in your life, than a necessary, must happen evil. Another part of this second reason is that people are afraid of the increased responsibilities that success brings. "Will I be able to sustain this higher level of success?" See, looping right back to the fear of failure. "Will people always be expecting more and more of me?" Here enters the sabotage thought, "It's better to just play it safe and not rock the boat of my life."

> **EVERYTHING IS A PROCESS**
>
> **GOAL SETTING IS THE BE ALL AND END ALL... NOT!**

Making goal setting into a habit can minimize the chances of your ever sabotaging your own success. In the movie, *What About Bob?* Bill Murray plays a neurotic's neurotic. What he needs to do is take "baby steps" to overcome fears. He was afraid to get on a bus, so he would take baby steps until he found himself on the bus.

Goal setting starts out as small, effective focusing on your monthly goals and gathers momentum to gradually improve your life and your success in life.

Two important messages here about the process of goal achievement, the process of mastery. 1) No quick fixes, and 2) no instant gratification. Goal setting is not the be all and end all. It is a foundational skill. Like all skills, it takes **time**. Here's my story on the path of mastering goal setting or on moving towards mastery.

I started setting goals down on a monthly basis over a decade ago. I fell into all of the pitfalls of a beginner. The first time I reviewed my progress on my first set of monthly goals proved to be extremely frustrating. The goals weren't very specific or measurable, I didn't know if I had hit them or not. I wasn't sure if they were really all that important ... I was one big lump of frustration. What made it even worse was that those that I was clear on, maybe I was achieving a third of them.

Great, what a goal setter! But I set down my next month's goals, and for the first six months or so, the same end of the month story of frustration. Specific? No. Measurable? No. Relevant? Maybe. No coach and still tracking at accomplishing 30 percent of what I was writing down. I was real close to giving up.

I kept my own advice, and just kept on keeping on. Sure enough, each month I did get my goals a little bit more specific and measurable, which helped immensely. At least now I knew whether I was hitting my goals or not. The first couple of months, at least for the first six months, I continued hitting a third of my goals. On some of them I still had no idea of how I was doing because of lack of specificity. Very discouraging, but I plowed forward.

Then for about a year and a half I hit a plateau of hitting 50 percent of what I was writing down and still no long term goals. Yes, I had some vague ideas, goals of some things I possibly wanted to achieve for myself, my family and for my career, but nothing with a deep down desire and conviction. These ideas would just come and go and would gather no head of steam.

Then it happened. After almost 4 years of dedicated goal setting, I started creating real breakthrough for my business and for what I saw as the direction of my life. It came down to just a few days. In those two to three days the thoughts, ideas, goals, vision just came to me very clearly. Nothing particularly mystical about it, just that all of my years of persistence, dedication, and just doing it, were paying off. The goal setting had been paying off well before these few days. It was just that my sense of who I was becoming was a lot clearer after this spurt of insight. Not that it all came to me in a completed picture, but definitely in a much clearer picture. A picture that I will certainly be fine tuning for the rest of my life.

The last five years I have been hitting 75-95 percent of the monthly's goals that I write down. After the last upward spike on my chart of successful goal achievement I have been on a very nice plateau. And I am definitely well positioned for the next wonderful breakthrough of higher and higher, more and more satisfying goal achievement.

It's back to the basic advice of just take care of your monthly goals, the "baby steps," if you will, of success. Your vision and your mission will unfold at their own pace and in their own good time. That's how a vision and a mission are created. I salute and honor the wonderful advice of beginning with the end in mind, but for many of the people that I work with, the end is too unclear, therefore there is no beginning, meaning no starting, or giving up too early on the goal achievement process, the G.A.P. Because when you do make a commitment to the goal achievement process, your monthly goals get more and more powerful, leading to a clearer vision, and a passionate, deep within your mind, and deep within your heart mission. Not a wishful thinking mission, but a mission that is S.M.A.R.T., balanced. Balancing the end in mind with what you choose to do today to move towards your dreams. Closing the gap between desire and actual results.

The Path of Mastery

I was introduced to George Leonard through an audiocassette program. George wrote a wonderful book about the path of mastery which the audio was based on. George has a great message. Beware of the illusion of the quick fix. Learn to love the plateau. Learn to love the plateau because it is an inevitable and necessary step on the path towards mastery.

George Leonard's chart for the path of mastery is a very effective way of looking at the learning curve. Whenever we learn something new, be it through a book, a seminar, a cassette program, we get all excited about the benefits we can expect from using these new strategies. We use the techniques, and sure enough there's an increase in effectiveness. Then the inevitable backslide occurs. The backslide is never quite as far back as before we learned the new approach. Then comes the inevitable plateau, where it seems as if we're going nowhere. But development of these new habits is being formed. Subtle little changes that we're probably not even aware of, that in their own due time, will create another positive, upward spike in our progress.

That's why it's so important to learn to love the plateau. Without this love, this respect for the process of growth, most people will give up on the process. Therefore they will not realize their potential because they gave up at the one-yard line. Gave up just before they created meaningful breakthrough in their life. I recommend that you read George Leonard's book, *Mastery*, to get the full, in depth explanation of how this process of the plateau works. George does a masterful job of this and gives us excellent insight into the path of mastery.

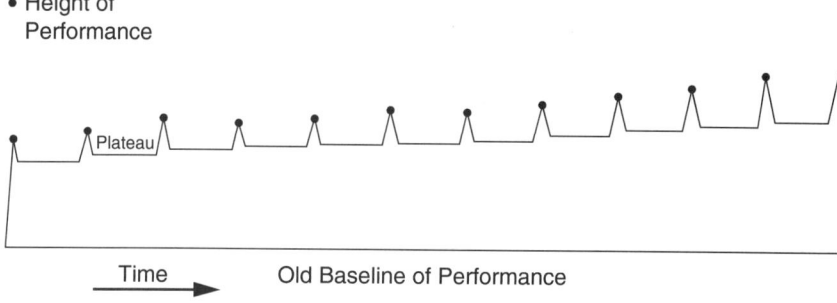

The Path of Mastery

Some Additional Tips

▸ Reasons

Take a form or the one provided in this book and list all the reasons why you want to achieve your goals. The principle here is a very simple one. The more reasons you have as to why you want to achieve your goals, the more motivation you're going to have to persist when the going gets tough.

A few reasons will give you some motivation. Twenty, 30, 50 or more reasons will make you unstoppable on your quest for balance and success. Examples of reasons could be: I have high self-esteem, I'm able to give more to my family, I'm able to give more to my community, I'm able to give more freely of my time and my money, I can do whatever I want, buy whatever I want, go wherever I want, with whom ever I want, whenever I want. Your list is limited only by your imagination. Like all of the other lists that we have generated, I recommend that you post your list where you can see it often—written and visible.

▶ Inspect What You Expect—Looking for a Few Good People

One more time. A crucial reminder of the importance of tracking your results and disciplining yourself to do what you choose to do. You choose to do these activities, these goals, because they are meaningful to you, because you know they will move you in the direction of your dreams.

With a coach or without a coach. Ideally you should have a coach, but it doesn't always work out ideally. This whole process can work by your tracking, monitoring yourself. With a coach, it's finding those few good people who really understand and are willing to make a commitment to this process.

The few good managers, coaches that I have come upon all say that the secret to their success with goal achievement is that they inspected what they expected with their monthly reviews. What we have been calling **"The Schwarzenegger Effect,"** or **"The General MacArthur Effect."**

What this review process does extremely effectively is not only squeeze out your full potential, it also squeezes out the B.S. you may be feeding yourself and your coach.

Getting your goals specific and measurable makes this squeezing possible. Remember, the easiest person to lie to in the world is yourself. Having your goals specific and measurable minimizes this type of lying. It helps your coach know when you're drawing upon your vast storehouse of excuses. A great coach will stop you from doing this. He will point out to you that you're running the risk of rationalizing away your success. He will get you back on and keep you on track. Without this "looking reality straight in the face" the goal achievement process is limp.

Inspecting what you expect also helps you identify your strengths and the areas that you need to develop. As you track what percentage of goals you're hitting, you'll be able to pinpoint what skills are lacking, those skills that are holding you back from hitting, accomplishing more of your goals. Once you have identified these areas of development, you can put together a very individualized training program to minimize and eliminate these weaknesses. Books, seminars, cassette programs and real world coaching to help you improve your skills.

Two Quotes

Careful of what you wish for, you might get it.

People plan and God laughs.

Every once in a while I meet people who have hit a particular goal, and they're not all that happy about it. Many times it has to do with a career move that they aspired to. They got the promotion(s) and are now not happy with their situation. Sometimes it has to do with family or relationship goals. Achieved, but not fulfilling.

Combine the monthly goal setting process with the fail forward wisdom. This means that by staying with the process, you minimize the risk of charging in the wrong direction. When and if you do "fail," be alert to the lessons to be learned.

The second quote is for those people who believe in a higher power and a cosmic plan. God's laughter is not at us, but the kind of laughter that comes with the wisdom of knowing what the ending holds for us. As I understand the laughter, it's about setting our sights, our plans, too low. God has greater plans for us, and perhaps we're just setting our goals too low. By staying with the process, our goals reach higher and higher. Our goals do become more of an expression of who we are in alignment with our greatest strengths to give and get for ourselves and our universal community.

NOW, DO IT!

If you haven't yet set down your first month's goals, set yourself a goal of when you're going to commit your goals to paper. One of my seminar participants alerted me to this type of goal. She told me, "Mark, my goal is to have my next month's goals written down by this Friday."

Back to a K.I.S.S.

If you remember nothing else that you have read, just remember and do this one thing. **Take 15-30 minutes once a month, to write down your upcoming months goals.**

This is how you begin the goal achievement process.

BECOME THE FEW WHO DO.

NOW, DO IT!

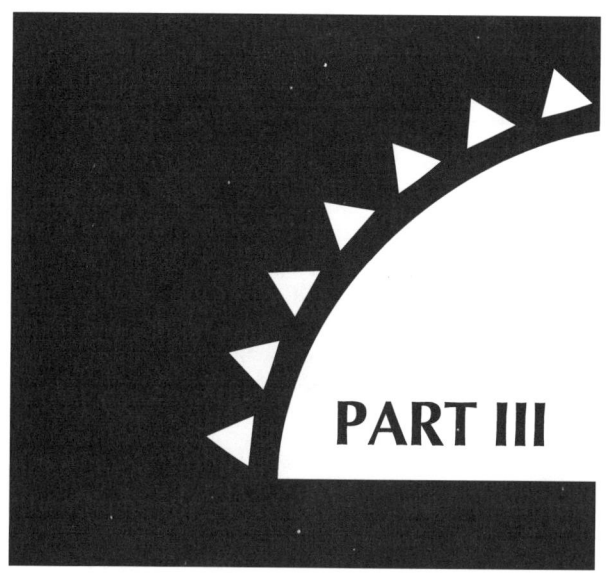

PART III

Time Management

Chapter Eight

Now, You Need Time Management

If you don't have goals, you don't need time management. Well, you do have goals, so now on to the management of your time.

Sometimes a prospective client will ask me to do a workshop on time management. One of my first questions to them is, "Are your people clear on their goals?" When I hear a response like, "Don't worry about goals, I'm sure they know what's expected of them. Just give us a session on time management." I do get worried. If their people aren't in fact clear on their goals, the workshop will probably be a waste of time. The company's just wasting its money. When you have S.M.A.R.T. goals, time management makes sense. Without goals, the strategies and techniques of time management will never maximize results and productivity.

86,400: Your Greatest Asset

Ever meet someone who's whining that there just aren't enough hours in the day? "There just isn't enough time for everything." Let's say by divine intervention this person was given two more hours in his day. What do you think he'll be saying when you meet him a year, or maybe even less than a year later? That's right. "Excuse me, can I have two more?"

What does the number 86,400 represent? My advance on this book? No. What I owe the IRS for this year's income? No (but some year soon . . . yes, I have the exact year written down). It's the number of seconds in a day. Nature is an Equal Opportunity Lender. No matter which of the seven continents you live on, this is your daily ration. No more, no less.

Time is funny that way. Everybody has all that there is, but nobody seems to have enough. In fact, time management itself is an oxymoron. Meaning, that no matter how well you manage it, 86,400 is all you get. So, let's get it straight, we won't really be talking about time management. Here are the higher levels of what time management really is all about, that we will be exploring:

Time Management

Choice/Decision Management

Priority Management

Stress Management

Self Management

Life Management

Just as I had two affirmations for the goal achievement process,

I advance confidently in the direction of my dreams.

I act as though it were impossible to fail.

I also have two affirmations pertaining to time management, which will be two central themes that we will be going over again and again in this section.

There is never enough time for everything, but there is always enough time for the most important thing.

Be ruthless with time, but gracious with people.

In the classic study on goal setting there were four questions:

- Do you believe that goals are important?
- Do you have goals?
- Do you write them down?
- Do you have an action plan for their accomplishment?

We've taken care of the first three questions. Now let's put our attention on the fourth question. And of course, we will continue in our great tradition of K.I.S.S.

I mention my re-commitment to keeping it short and simple at this point because a lot of people start to moan and groan when they think of putting together an action plan—thick binders with many hours invested into the planning. Draft after draft submitted for final approval, and then even further fine tuning of the plan after approval. For a business plan, an annual strategic plan, this certainly can be the case.

My recommended action planning will take you 5-10 minutes a day, five days of the week. That is at first. After a while, meaning once it has become a habit (there's that word again), your investment in yourself is several seconds a day.

My strength is the daily tactical approach. I don't specialize in helping companies or individuals put together their strategic plans, their individual business plans. I specialize in helping companies and individuals **implement** their plans. Helping them to get clearer on their **mission goals** and the critical **how to goals.**

I find that most companies do a great job of putting together very sophisticated, very well thought out plans. Then they don't implement, don't take action on these great plans. Too often these plans end up on somebody's credenza or disappear into a file folder, not to reappear until performance appraisal time. Looking at your plan once or twice a year is not enough. Often it's too late to make any significant corrections, adjustments to the plan.

Going the Distance

The great part about the daily planning commitment is, like the monthly goal setting commitment, the total is greater than the sum of the parts. In goal setting the monthly commitment leads to vision and mission. In daily planning the commitment leads to becoming a business plan, a strategic plan. Eventually, perhaps even a plan for your life.

Your business plan doesn't end up being just a frustrating experience, but a document that is kept alive throughout the year by your daily and monthly planning. The business plan becomes a document that does lead to increased productivity, just as planned.

Carpe Diem

Carpe Diem is the Latin term for "Seize the Day," and as you astute movie goers know from the movie that Robin Williams starred in, *Dead Poets Society.*

In the movie, Professor Keating, played by Robin Williams, also called by his more daring students, "O captain, my captain," urged his students, "make your lives extraordinary" by seizing the day—a day that is that step in a thousand mile journey.

The Greatest Story Ever Told ... About Time Management

Back around the turn of the twentieth century, the president of Bethlehem Steel had a vision and a mission. His name was Charles Schwab, and this is his story of how he seized the day to realize his goals, dreams, vision and mission.

First let me give you the end that he had in mind. He had a vision of getting Andrew Carnegie and J.P. Morgan together and then influencing them to form US Steel, which was his mission. He used the greatest management principle, seizing the day, to accomplish his goals, vision and mission. Here's his story.

Charles Schwab's boss was Andrew Carnegie. Mr. Carnegie attributed his success to his uncanny ability to surround himself with talented people. He knew how to hire people who knew how to hire people. The right people. People with that great balance of talent and attitude. Schwab realized early on that he needed to do the same thing. He needed not only to surround himself with the right people, he needed to train himself and his people in the greatest management principles.

The cornerstone of Schwab's mission to create US Steel was to make Bethlehem Steel into a world power. This would be his leverage point to influence Mr. Carnegie and Mr. Morgan. And to accomplish this, he first had to learn the greatest management principles and then have these principles taught to his vice presidents.

To help him in this quest, he was referred to a management consultant out of Manhattan by the name of Ivy Lee. Charles invited Ivy to come out to Bethlehem and to teach him the greatest management principles. When Ivy came out to Bethlehem, PA, he spent just 15 minutes with Charles Schwab. Fifteen minutes that would change the way Charles would manage himself and his people forever.

Ivy Lee started simply enough. After Charles explained what he wanted to accomplish with Bethlehem Steel and with his VPs, Ivy suggested where they needed to start.

He recommended to Charles that every night, just before he left work for the day, he would need to take 5-10 minutes to prepare for the next day. Just take a blank piece of paper, put the next day's date at the top of the page, and then write down the six most important things that he needed to accomplish that next day. Once these six were written down, he would need to prioritize them into their respective A, B and C priorities. "A" being a "must do". "B" being a "should do" and "C" being a "nice to do". A "must do" is non-negotiable. It's critical to have this activity completed or at least started on that day. Once you have completed these "A" priorities, then you can move onto your "B's," "C's" if time allows. One other piece of advice from Mr. Lee, "Start with your # 1 priority. When you're finished with that, move on to your next priority."

Some of you may be thinking, "Yeah, right, that might work in the ideal world, but in my work environment, no way. Start with # 1, and then when completed, on to # 2. Give me a break. What about all the interruptions? What about the shifting/changing priorities? What about all the things that implode on my time? I have my daily plan all laid out, and as soon as I walk through my office door or venture into the world, everything seems to be coming my way, and my plan is thrown right out the window."

Fear not. We will address all of these concerns. First we need to get the principle of taking the time to plan for the next day in place. Then I promise we will address the "real world."

So at this point, Ivy Lee started to leave Charles Schwab's office, getting ready to go back to Manhattan. Charles asked him where he was going. When he heard he was heading on out, Schwab asked him two questions. "Is that it?" and "What do I owe you?"

Ivy Lee said, "That's it for the day." As for what he owed him—two things. One Charles owed himself—to make a commitment to doing this 5-10 minute exercise five times a week for the next three months, Sunday night through Thursday night, just before he left work (except for Sunday), take the 5-10 minutes to plan for the next day. If due to circumstances or personal preference, he wanted to plan first thing in the morning for the upcoming day, fine. But be sure to make the time to plan on this daily basis.

The reason for the three month commitment was that Ivy knew that this was how long it would take for this exercise to become a habit—a habit being where something is easier to do than not do. Ivy explained that until this daily planning became a habit, it would be premature to start teaching any other management principles. Because without this one crucial habit in place, the other management techniques would prove to be ineffective, or at least not as effective as they could and would be with this daily planning habit in place.

And as for what Charles owed Ivy, "At the end of the three months, send me a check for what you think this idea was worth to you."

Three months later, Ivy Lee received a check from Charles Schwab for $25,000.00! Remember, this was in the 1890's. In today's money, that's about $700,000.00! For 15 minutes of consulting work. Good thing for Charles that Ivy didn't charge him his daily rate. In his autobiography, Charles Schwab, who indeed did have his vision and mission fulfilled through the creation of US Steel, said that of all the management principles he had ever learned, the discipline of planning for the next day the night before was the most important strategy that he ever used and was the basis for the effectiveness of the other techniques that he would learn.

Speaking of turn of the century money, let me share with you some fascinating history that I learned about Carnegie, Morgan and Schwab while watching a recent *A&E Biography* special about Andrew Carnegie.

While putting Andrew Carnegie's estate together, shortly after his death, a crumbled old piece of paper was discovered in a desk where he did much of his work. On this piece of paper were written three goals, written many years before Mr. Carnegie achieved his phenomenal financial success. His first goal was to live to be ninety, the second goal was to become one of the wealthiest men in the world, and the third goal was to spend every single penny of it. He achieved all three.

He lived to the age of 85 (we'll call this close enough to his age goal), and when he was 65, he became the richest man in the world when J.P. Morgan bought his steel empire. The last twenty years were spent spending his entire fortune on philanthropic pursuits.

Here's a little more detail on the last two goals. The meeting between Carnegie and Morgan, and the merging of their steel empires had been influenced by Charles Schwab, as he had intended many years before. Mr. Morgan expressed great interest to Mr. Carnegie in the buying of his steel empire and wanted to know if he was interested in selling. Carnegie asked for one day to think about it, that he would give Morgan his answer the next day. When they got back together, Carnegie said that he would sell to Morgan. When Morgan asked for how much, Carnegie simply slid a piece of paper over to Morgan. Morgan unfolded the paper, looked at the figure penciled down by Carnegie, looked up at Carnegie and said, "Congratulations, you are now the richest man in the world." The figure that they had so quickly agreed upon was $440,000,000.00. Again, to put this in today's earning perspective, that's about $12.5 billion dollars!

And he did spend every penny of it. He set up a fund for his wife for $40 million. The rest went to the formation of the Carnegie Foundation in New York, the endowment of several universities, and the funding of most of the American library system. Between America and England, 1700 libraries benefited. No money was left to his heirs. The present day Carnegies have no money from their ancestor's fortune. Just as he had planned.

Oh, what about Charles Schwab? What was in it for him? He was US Steel's first president.

I'm Against Using "To Do" Lists

So with all that I have said about daily planning, let it be known that I'm 100 percent against using a "To Do" list.

With tongue in cheek.

A "To Do" list is where you just have a lot of activities listed, without the distinguishing of higher priorities from lower priorities. Without this distinction, you run the risk of becoming one of those chickens running around with its head cut off—just reacting to whatever comes your way. No plan, just busy . . . but not effective, not maximizing your results.

I do believe in the power of making lists. In fact there's a saying that goes, "When you're feeling listless, make a list." One of the people whom I coach told me that she was having what she called, "a free floating guilt weekend." She was definitely feeling guilty, but she just wasn't sure what she was feeling guilty about. Her energy was really low, and the whining was sky high. So she took the bull by the horns. She sat down and wrote out all of the things that she was putting off, both at work and in her home. Then she picked out a few of the more important tasks that she could get right to. By the end of the day, the free floating guilt was gone, and several important projects were taken care of.

I'm a great believer in "what gets written gets done." She knew that there were important things she kept putting off, and just by writing it down and crystallizing it, clarifying it in her mind, the guilt clouds parted, the energy level went up, the procrastinating stopped.

So yes, I'm against a "To Do" list, but I'm for a "Daily Priority List." Meaning a list where you're crystal clear on which are the relevant activities and where you need to discipline yourself to do first things first. Too many people "major in minors" and are not involved in "the vital few," because they're trapped by "the trivial many."

Stephen Covey in *The 7 Habits of Highly Effective People* said it best. "It is more important to schedule your priorities, than to prioritize your schedule." Prioritizing your schedule without being clear on what the priorities are is an exercise in futility. It leads to being activity, not priority driven. "The main thing is to keep the main thing the main thing." Or as Peter Drucker, the founder of modern management thinking puts it, "Management by Objectives

(MBO) definitely works. Unfortunately 90 percent of the time people are not aware of the objectives."

The 80/20 Rule: Coming Back to a K.I.S.S.

Every evening, night or morning take 5-10 minutes to plan for the upcoming day. A "Daily Priority List" works because of the application of the 80/20 rule, also know as the *Pareto Principle*.

Pareto, an Italian economist around the turn of the twentieth century, discovered that 80 percent of the world's wealth was in the hands of 20 percent of the population. Then when he looked at an industry's product line, he found that 80 percent of the sales came from 20 percent of the products. Also, 80 percent of the sales were coming from 20 percent of the sales force, and pertaining to time management, **80 percent of your productivity comes from 20 percent of your activity.** Good news! Great news! So, forget about getting through everything on your list. Just make sure that you're clear on your priorities. Separate them into their respective "A's," "B's," and "C's," and break it down even further into "A1, A2, A3, B1, B2" etc.

For instance, let's say that you have 10 items on your list. The Pareto Principle tells us that two of those things on your list will be responsible for 80 percent of your effectiveness. As we have been discussing all along, be clear on your high impact, doing what counts, relevant activities. And to enhance this process further, get a coach involved to help you remain objective and on target concerning which are truly your top priorities.

You've just come off another extremely demanding and full day, and once again you were only able to get to two things on your daily priority list. But which two were they? Yes, the two that got you 80 percent of your productivity. As for the day, all things being unequal, this was the best you could do. And it's the best that you did.

I don't know of too many busy, highly successful people who ever get through all of the things on their list. But they are always crystal clear on what the highest priority activities are. It's a bit like the goal setting process. I have **never** hit 100 percent of my goals in any given month. But every month I am crystal clear on where I need to put my attention to maximize my results. Every month I'm maximizing on my opportunities, either achieving them or at least making great progress towards accomplishing my goals. Same credo for the day, not getting to everything, but making great headway towards everything that remains important—important being defined as anything that moves me towards my goals.

No Whining, No Trying, No Guilt . . . Everybody Is a Procrastinator

I read that 50 percent of people are procrastinators, and the other 50 percent live or work with someone who is a procrastinator. Everybody is touched by this thief of time, procrastination. I believe that everybody procrastinates. Before I get into that, let's define what we mean by procrastination.

Following the lead of Mark Twain, "Never put off until tomorrow, what you can put off until the day after tomorrow." Or remember that great procrastinator, Norton, played by Art Carney from the TV show "The Honeymooners?" Before he would start an activity, he would go through all kinds of funny hand and body gyrations. You got the feeling that this would go on forever, if it weren't for Ralph, played by Jackie Gleason, finally shouting/yelling out, "Norton. Will you cut that out!"

A lot of people I meet feel guilty about the fact that they see themselves as procrastinators. A lot of people also feel guilty about the clutter in their lives, which we will cover later.

I believe that everybody is a procrastinator. We all procrastinate on some things, and that is the key to what I believe. Everybody procrastinates, but the issue here is what are you procrastinating about? The 20 percent that is going to get you 80 percent of your productivity? Or are you procrastinating on the 80 percent that will only get you 20 percent of your potential productivity?

I'm always procrastinating on the 80 percent. Stretching a few of the 80 percent until the last possible moment. Not all 80 percent, but definitely always a few things hanging around to get done. So what? For me, it's an issue of a "reality check." Are you ever 100 percent caught up on everything? Maybe once or twice in your life. Are you ever caught up on all of the most important things? For me, yes, at least 80 percent of the time, probably closer to 90-98 percent of the time. Don't procrastinate on the 20 percent that is going to get you your 80 percent productivity. Definitely cut yourself some slack on the other 80 percent, so that you're not driving yourself and the people around you crazy, with your obsessive pursuit of perfection. The operative word here is obsessive. No problem, shooting for the ideal, striving for perfection, but don't drag your day and your life down with you while you're going after this unattainable state of perfection. Even great time managers are busy, rush around occasionally and do procrastinate.

So, There Are Just Two Things to Know, and Do

It's either this . . . [see the picture of a chicken on page 109], or this [see the picture of a path with detours.]

The choice is yours. And there are two disciplines to help you with this:

1. Take 15-30 minutes once a month to set your upcoming month's goals, review the previous month's achievements.
2. Take 5-10 minutes at the end of your work day to plan for your next day.

Hey, give it a chance! Do it. You'll like the results.

Remember, there are two pains in life, the pain of discipline and the pain of regret. I know which one you will choose. The good news is that the pain of discipline is not very painful.

Oh, about re-doing lists. Simply keep a running list. There is no need to write up a new list every day. Have great fun marking/checking/crossing off those you have finished. I know people who love crossing things off of their list so much that they take a big, thick, black marker to run it through the completed task. They say it intensifies the satisfaction of completion.

With a running list, maybe every other week, you'll need to consolidate all of your priorities onto a fresh list. This will get you refocused and keep your list manageable instead of flipping through too many pages. How often you need to do this is your call. Go with your instincts on this one. You'll know when things are getting a little out of focus because of a run-on list.

In this information/computer age, contact management software is also effective. The best known software packages are Goldmine, Maximizer and ACT.

> THERE IS NEVER ENOUGH TIME FOR EVERYTHING, BUT THERE IS ALWAYS ENOUGH TIME FOR THE MOST IMPORTANT THING.

THIS?

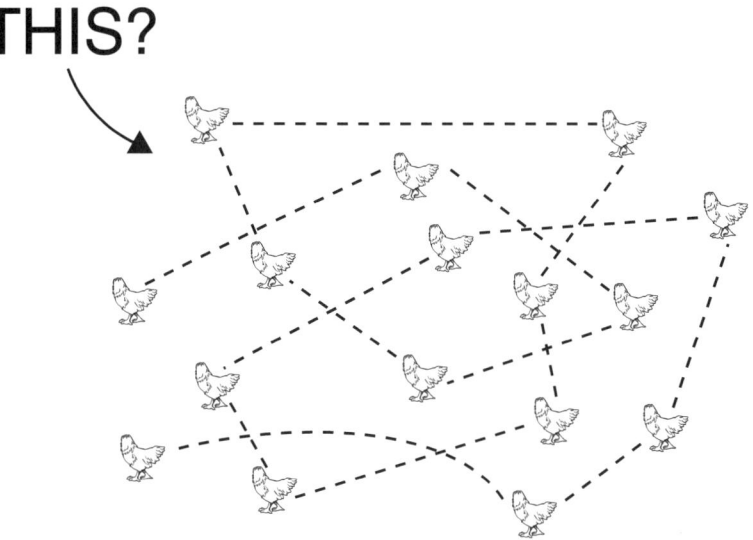

Chicken running around with its head cut off.

OR THIS?

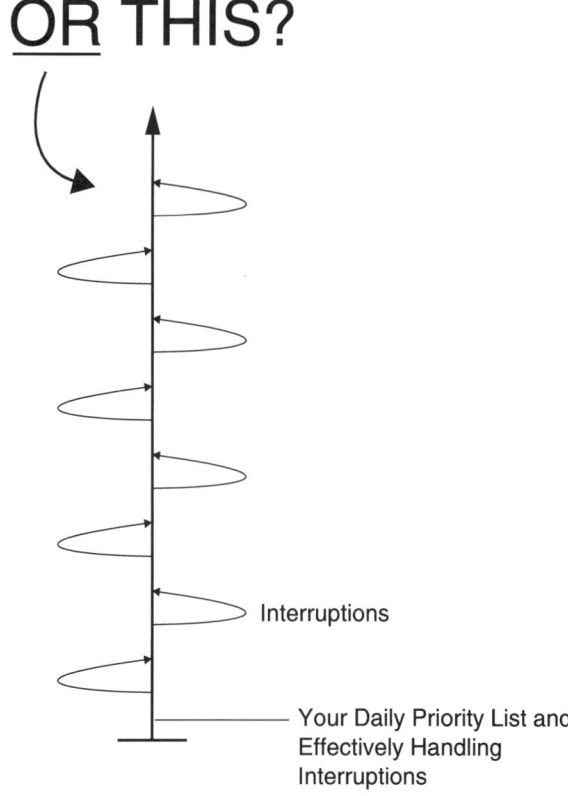

Interruptions

Your Daily Priority List and Effectively Handling Interruptions

CHAPTER NINE

Minimizing & Eliminating Time Wasters, Plus How to Handle Those Interruptions

Now, we have taken an important step in knowing how to manage our greatest asset . . . time. We know that no matter how focused we are, how well we "manage" our time, it is just not possible to have enough time to get to everything. But because of the power and the wisdom of the 80/20 rule, we know we don't need to get to everything. We simply need to know and get to our most important priorities. **There is always** enough time for the most important things in our life.

Be Ruthless With Time, But Gracious With People. Now, On to Handling Interruptions

As the daily priority list path shows us, even with a great plan, a clear vision, an inspiring mission, we'll still be taken off the path by the slings and arrows of every day interruptions.

What we want to do is minimize the distractions. As soon as we effectively handle these intrusions, we come back to the path of our written priorities.

Time now for me to keep my promise to you of addressing the real world of planning. The advice is to plan out your day. Start with your first priority, and when that's completed, move on to your next priority, and so forth. Well, it doesn't quite work out that way. We have our day all planned out, and we encounter one distraction, one interruption after another.

I know of several executives who wake up early and work at home for an hour and a half or so. They report that they get a tremendous amount of quality work accomplished, and then they go to work at the office, to be interrupted throughout the day.

Research shows that in an 8-12 hour business day, on the average you will be interrupted 73 times which translates to once every 6-9 minutes. I told one of my clients about this research, and she said, "I'll take that!" Meaning that she feels that she gets interrupted even more than the research indicates!

So interruptions are a fact of life. What we will do now is address those things that waste your time and introduce you to dozens of time management techniques that will help you to minimize and eliminate interruptions, help you to cut down on the amount of time that the interruptions are holding you captive. I'll teach you how to be ruthless with your time while remaining gracious to the people with whom you work. Certainly you don't want to become a great time manager while alienating the people that are on your team.

Time Wasters

What is a time waster? Any time that your attention shifts from a high priority task to a low priority task. That simple.

The four areas that are the most common time wasters are:

- Lack of planning/Lack of goal setting
- Lack of personal organization/Lack of self-discipline
- Lack of self-management
- Lack of control over the work environment

Take this short exercise to start to identify what are your biggest time wasters.

Step I is to circle all of the time wasters that you feel are true for you. **Note:** You are not allowed to circle all of them!

Step II is to look at those that you circled and pick out your top five, and then rank them #1-5, with #1 being your biggest time waster.

Step III is to put together an action plan that will help you to start to minimize the effect of these time wasters and to eventually eliminate them. After going through this exercise I will introduce you to over fifty time management techniques to help you put together a personalized and powerful action plan for the elimination of these time wasters.

Time Wasters

Circle your top time wasters.

1. Lack of written goals that are S.M.A.R.T. Lack of focus.
2. No coach to help you with your S.M.A.R.T. goals
3. Indecision, poor at making decisions
4. Snap decisions
5. Attempting to do too much
6. Too many goals
7. Failure to break priorities into smaller manageable parts
8. Lack of a plan for meeting goals
9. Lack of daily priorities, of using a Daily Priority List
10. Shifting priorities, jumping from one to another
11. Poor crisis management, fire fighting too often
12. A lack of dated checkpoints to assess progress, lack of feedback
13. Poor use of "waiting time"
14. Travel
15. Poor geographical planning of appointments
16. Making poor time estimates of how long something will take to get done, unrealistic time frames
17. Personal disorganization, cluttered desk, poor filing, misplaced items
18. Procrastination
19. Leaving tasks unfinished
20. Taking on projects you don't have the necessary skills for
21. Lack of delegation, trying to do everything yourself
22. Ineffective delegation
23. Perfectionism
24. Inability to say "NO"
25. Socializing, too much idle chatter
26. Failure to take notes
27. Haste or impatience
28. Absenteeism or late too often
29. Negative attitudes
30. Lack of self-discipline
31. Fatigue, low energy
32. Telephone/voice mail/e-mail interruptions
33. Unexpected drop-in visitors
34. Paper work, red tape, too many memos, unnecessary correspondence
35. Meetings (high frequency, low quality), too many appointments
36. Meetings without goals, appointments without goals
37. Incomplete, unclear, inaccurate or waiting for information
38. Poor staff, or not enough staff
39. Inadequate resources, inadequate equipment
40. Poor communication with supervisor or support staff
41. Poor listening skills

42. Confused responsibility or lack of authority to implement decisions
43. Overcontrol by boss or bosses

Now, rank #1-5 your top 5 time wasters

Knowing For Sure . . . Log It

The above exercise is just a guess at what's wasting your time. If you want to know for sure what's wasting your time, keep a time log for five business days. Simply write down everything that you do on those days with the amount of time that you spend doing it.

Yes, I know that keeping a time log is not for everyone, but some people will discipline themselves to do this, and the benefits are well worth the investment of time. And as with everything else that I have recommended, this is easy to do. I hear people whining about keeping a time log all of the time. "It wastes my time to keep a log to figure out what's wasting my time." This is just another one of those excuses. It's easy to do, and you don't need to obsess and drive yourself crazy over this log. Just write down everything, and also write down the amount of time spent on the task.

Since there is no such thing as a normal day, or a normal week, the five business days of a time log should span two weeks. Wednesday-Friday in week one, and Monday-Tuesday in week two. As you can see, I'll suggest anything to minimize whining.

Keeping a time log will help you further fine tune knowing what really is wasting your time. Most time management guru's, especially in the 1960's through the 1980's, enthusiastically promoted the idea of keeping a time log. Like most of these techniques, they were actually done by very few people. If you are inclined to believe that a time log will be of great benefit to you, become the few who do. The benefit is more accurately knowing what the time wasters are, which leads to putting your attention in the right areas. Your quest to minimize and eliminate time wasters from your life will be more effective. Knowing the correct time wasters for yourself will lead to picking out the right strategies and time management techniques to use to maximize results.

Time Management Techniques, Saving Two Hours a Day

Time is our greatest asset.

Because without time, we don't have a field of action, a field wherein we can achieve our dreams and goals. We need to know and use strategies and techniques that will allow us to best utilize our 86,400 seconds per day, 168 hours per week, 525,600 minutes (a great song from **"Rent"**) per year. We are now going to discuss these techniques.

I have heard time management consultants say that by using these techniques people can expect to save up to two hours a day, meaning that what used to take you 10 hours to do will now take you only 8. And I have also heard some of these gurus say that saving two hours a day is very conservative. For some disciplined individuals the savings can be phenomenally greater.

One important point about this saving of time. It doesn't come in huge blocks. What you will do is save three minutes here, another minute there, 17 minutes using this technique, four minutes using that technique. The point is that these techniques help save you small bits of time which add up to a significant saving of time over the course of a day, a month, a year, a lifetime. So, that's our reality check concerning saving time. Look to save a moment here and a minute there. Don't be looking for one or two of these techniques to give you that quick fix of time salvation.

Here's a further illustration of what we mean about saving time. One of the areas that wastes time is lack of control over the work environment. Here's what the research has to say about the wasting of time in this realm.

The Phone

An average planned call takes 7 minutes. An average unplanned call, an interruption, takes 12 minutes. In each case the call's objective was met, but one took 5 minutes longer than the other. If you make or take 10 planned calls, versus taking 10 interrupted calls in a day, that's 50 minutes that you saved. I know that important and effective, unplanned phone calls do happen, but the research indicates that if you have made a habit of not planning calls or not planning when to make or take calls, you run the risk of wasting time.

Drop-In Visitors

The average drop-in visitor will take up to 10 minutes of your time. When you are clear on your priorities, and know how to say "no", this same drop-in will be effectively handled in 2 minutes. After highlighting a few of these "saving a few minutes at a time" examples, we'll go into greater depth on how to use these time management techniques. So please be patient with me. You will see how all of these techniques will help you to be, as we promised, ruthless with time, but gracious with people.

Meetings

Unstructured meetings take twice as much time as planned meetings. A planned thirty minute meeting, if unplanned, will take one hour to get the same results.

In fact, your top three time wasters alone will waste up to two hours of your time a day.

Strategies & Techniques for Handling Interruptions, and for Eliminating Time Wasters

I'm going to run a whole bunch of techniques by you right now. In no particular order, or priority. **As you read through them, circle/ highlight/underline those that look as if they would be helpful to you.** After you read through them all, I'll explain what to do with the ones that you have highlighted.

Look at your top time wasters again. This will help you remember where you need the most help. We're going to discuss the six most common time waster problems. Those that apply to people worldwide and are not industry specific. Your job is to pick out the problems and the techniques that specifically relate to your situation. Time management is a very personal thing. As the saying goes, "One person's meat is another person's poison." So, as always, no cookie cutter approaches. Find what makes sense for you in the next couple of pages, and then set some goals to use those techniques that speak directly to your time management challenges and time management style.

Speaking of style, there are two basic time management styles, 1) basically orderly, where for these people time management is nothing more than a common sense approach, and staying well organized is no big deal. It comes easy to them. 2) basically disorderly—where the person has to put some effort into staying organized and never seems to quite get there. I'm from the basically orderly style.

I recommend that you listen to a single 60 minute audiocassette by Dru Scott, Ph.D.; *How to Put More Time in Your Life*, which can be ordered through Nightingale-Conant Corporation, at 1-800-525-9000. Dru does an excellent job of describing the different time management styles. She gives you some great strategies on how to best handle each type's own unique challenges.

Here are the most common time management problems, with a few solutions:

Problem: Personal Disorganization, Lack of Self-Discipline

Solutions:

1. Recognize that a cluttered desk **can be** a major interrupter. I highlighted "can be" because I believe that there should be a sign that says, "A messy desk is the sign of a messy desk."

Remember, no guilt! Just because you're surrounded by stacks and stacks of paper and post-its doesn't automatically qualify you as cluttered and disorganized. I have walked into some offices that if a hurricane whipped through them, they probably would have created an 80% improvement. But I found some of these people not to be cluttered. And I have walked into other offices that were squeaky clean and found some of these people to be extremely cluttered and disorganized.

Clutter's Last Stand

Let's better understand what clutter is, and is not.
Being organized *is not*:

- The same thing as being neat. Being messy and being organized have nothing to do with each other.
- It is not a moral issue. If you think, or feel that you are a messy, disorganized person, this doesn't mean that you are a bad person or that there is something deep down in your soul fundamentally wrong with you. Feeling guilty is not appropriate!
- It is not about being perfect. More on perfectionism in a few pages.

Being organized *is*:

- Being able to find things when you want to find them.
- Getting done what you want to get done when you want to get it done.
- Effectively concentrating on and achieving your goals!

So, if you can concentrate on the thing that you're working on and can find things when you want to find them, you're not cluttered, regardless of what your space looks like.

Concentration, meaning that you are able to focus your attention on what you're working on. Too many people tell me that they're working on one thing and then looking at a second and a third stack of paper. Now they're working on all three, or more, and not concentrating on any of them. This leads to ineffective results.

Finding things. Sometimes I meet people with stacks of paper and things all over the place, and when they need a certain document, they walk right over to a huge pile, look 2/3's of the way down the pile, and there's what they're looking for.

When I say having trouble finding things, I'm not talking about once in a while, but several times a day, several days a week. Wasting time looking for things. Clutter alone can waste between 30 minutes to an hour of your time a day. Get rid of clutter as we have defined it.

There are eight areas of clutter.

1. *Mental Clutter.* Trying to think thirty-seven or two thoughts at once. Nature has given us the ability to think one thought at a time. Cramming thoughts together causes lack of focus, indecision, conflict, headaches (that big vein in the middle of the forehead really gets throbbing), chickens running around with their heads cut off, leading to a crazed, burned out, overwhelmed individual.

2. *Calendar Clutter.* Appointments stacking up back-to-back causing stress and lowered productivity. And now with e-calendars people have access to your calendar and may schedule themselves onto your calendar with little regard for your time needs.

3. *Interpersonal Clutter.* Ever notice that 85 percent of your problems talk back to you? Or that your first five problems of the day all have first names? You need someone else's cooperation to help you achieve your goals, and all you're doing is ignoring or yelling at them.

4. *Team Clutter.* People not clear on expectations, not clear on goals, people pulling and being pulled in several different directions. Being on hold with your goals because you're waiting for someone on another team, in another division, who hasn't met his deadline, hasn't kept his promise to get you something on time. Priorities always changing. No clear vision, no clear purpose or mission as a team.

These next three are closely tied together:

5. *Paper Clutter*

6. *Desk Clutter*

7. *Space Clutter*

The 6 S's of Paper, Desk and Space Clutter

When it comes to paper, I've met these different types. Some people are cursed with all six, some with several, some with only one. See if you can relate to one, some, or all of these.

Stuffers—These are the people who, when they open their desk drawers, it's like a jack-in-the-box. They open the drawer and stuff comes popping out, or they can't even get the drawer open. I mean a junk drawer is all right, but do they all have to be junk drawers?

Stackers—Stacks and stacks of paper everywhere. These people are afraid of "out of sight out of mind". So they keep lots of stuff visible on their desks. People throughout the world suffer from piles!

Spreaders—Paper, paper everywhere. Spread all over the desk and migrating onto the tops of file cabinets, credenzas and even chairs. Ever walk into someone's office and because of "spreading" there's no place to sit?

Slingers—Now onto the floor go the papers. Desk full, every bit of furniture covered. So now onto the floor. The rug covered wall-to-wall. Good thing they don't start slinging fly paper. Could you imagine?

Savers—They can't throw anything away! Like their cousins, the stackers, who need to keep things within eyes range, these people hold onto everything, because, who knows, they might need it someday! A client recently showed me a note from his ex-wife that said, "Meet me at Woodstock."

Stickers—Those wonderful but sometimes grossly overused post-its. Several nice rows of color coordinated stickers going down the side of the desk or on a bathroom mirror. Stickers on phones, faxes, computers, steering wheels, backs of palms, collars, ties, chins, and eventually foreheads. Reminds me of when I was in kindergarten and either my parents or my teacher would pin something onto my shirt so I wouldn't forget.

These six S's add up to one other S—**Stuff!** The comedian, George Carlin, has a great comedy routine about stuff. He says that people eventually have so much stuff that they have to move into bigger homes just to hold all of their stuff. Stuff moving from their desks, out into the hallways, into their cars, closets and eventually into their homes.

P.S. I've recently been alerted to additional S's! Specifically **shufflers and sorters**. In the AM papers on the left side of the desk, mid-desk by mid-day, and on the right side of the desk by late afternoon. Shuffling around papers, sorting through the papers, **but nothing getting done! No action being taken.**

8. *Computer Clutter.* Not a date base but a data mess. Desk tops, lap tops, palm tops, and more to come soon. You experience the power of the information age only when you can access information easily, efficiently and effectively. Without information being properly organized, it can only lead to frustration and lower productivity.

Some Solutions

The Four D's

The 80/20 rule also applies to paperwork. By using this one simple technique it will minimize clutter and the S's. The principle is that 80 percent of paperwork can be touched once and be done with. Unfortunately, poor habits have people touching only 20 percent of their paperwork once. Which means, 60 percent of paperwork is unnecessarily being recycled and aggravating clutter and the six S's.

When you're picking up a piece of paper, or going through your in-box, develop the habit of thinking of the four D's. Here are the four D's:

Do: Can I take some action on this now? Write a quick memo/response on the paper, place a call, send a fax or an e-mail?

Delay: Yes, I need to take action on this, but not right now. Put the paper into your tickler filing system or enter it into your contact management software as a reminder of when to take action.

Delegate: Decide whom you can delegate it to and when. Start a "To Delegate" list of what to delegate, to whom and by when.

Tips on Delegating

1. Plan before you delegate
   - Don't delegate what you can eliminate
   - Don't waste other people's time with trivial items
   - Don't waste your time with trivial items
   - If possible, give multiple delegations at one time

2. Decide who does it
    - Use "Situational Delegation" skills. Some you supervise closely, others you leave alone.
    - Delegate to people according to the ability and availability
3. Communicate the details
    - Give enough information
    - Set deadline dates
    - Whenever possible, do it in person
    - Delegate authority as well as responsibility
4. Manage and evaluate
    - Establish times for review and schedule the reviews
    - Resist the tendency to have things delegated back to you!
5. Reward successful completion
    - Of all work finished on target and on time
    - Praise can often be the most effective reward
    - Handwritten "Thanks" for a job well done

As Dan Sullivan advises in a book that I highly recommend, *The Strategic Coach*, delegate everything except your unique genius, your unique talents. Put together a unique team where each team member is focused on using his greatest strengths.

> **Drop:** A persons best friend is a wastebasket. If you don't need it, throw it away! In my Step-By-Step, "How to Get Uncluttered List" I recommend that the truly cluttered wheel a dumpster into their office or hallway.
>
> This D also stands for **Delete**. Don't save up all of those unnecessary voice and e-mails. Eighty percent of them can be deleted, thereby reducing your mental clutter.

Can you see how these four can minimize or eliminate clutter and the S's'?

The S.W.A.T. Team

This team can be made up of people entirely from your company, a team of consultants or a combination of the best of both worlds ...some team members...some consultants.

People in your company who are **subject matter experts** in a particular area can give advice to people who are cluttered in that area. For example, someone at your company is excellent at keeping his paper, files, desk and office space well organized. He would share his trade secrets with those "spacially challenged" and help them get started on the road toward sanity.

Or you can bring in an outside consultant like me to help with mental or calendar clutter. I have associates in my SWAT team to help with interpersonal, team, paper, desk, space or computer clutter. My most popular associate (in terms of being called in to help) specializes in helping my clients unclutter their paper, desk and space. In four hours or less she'll have your office sparkling and organized with systems in place to keep it that way. It's beautiful seeing the wide smiles on people's faces as she rolls away the dumpsters and captures your near perfect office with before and after camera shots.

Here are some more solutions for the personal disorganization problem/challenge.

    2. Use a complete "all in one place" time organizer system. All in one place meaning the organizer has:

- A monthly calendar
- Daily Priority Lists (1-31's)
- A place to take and retrieve notes
- A place for your most important phone numbers/addresses

The three time organizers that I see most often are:

- Franklin Quest, 800-654-1776 (1776, nice touch)
- Daytimers, 800-225-5005
- Priority Manager (which I use), 800-665-1133
  (I also see Dayrunner, and Time Systems a lot.)

These time organizers are not for everybody. Yes, everybody **could** benefit from them, if they **use** them. Too often, I see people going to workshops on how to use these systems that probably shouldn't be going. These are excellent, well thought out seminars, but then they don't use the system. If you feel that you are someone who could benefit from these systems and will use them, call the above numbers, get their catalog, and pick out the organizer that works best for you.

    3. Tackle the toughest, highest priority task first. This is right out of the advice that Ivy Lee gave to Charles Schwab. Ideally, you do start the day with your top priority, but it doesn't always work

out that way, depending on circumstances. A client once asked me if I started every day off with my first priority. The answer is no, but I am crystal clear every day about what my top priority is, and some time during the day I do get to it.

4. Plan your work. Work your plan. A saying that has been around for a long time. Just as true and applicable today as it was years ago. Great wisdom . . . think about it . . . so simple. Plan your work/set some goals and objectives . . . then work your plan. **Do what you say you're going to do.** Integrity. Character. Discipline. Just do it.

5. Set goals, priorities, and deadlines. A deadline is a lifeline. It creates a sense of urgency. Goals, priorities, and deadlines become your organizing principle.

6. Replace bad habits with good ones. **You can change.** Remember the Popeye Syndrome? Don't be one of those who say, "I am what I am." You are, but we can all improve and better ourselves. Personal disorganization and lack of self-discipline are some bad habits that we have gotten into. Change . . . by using these different strategies and techniques, especially the strategies of monthly goal setting and daily prioritizing.

7. Discipline yourself to follow through. Let nothing important slip through the cracks. Following through and completing tasks raises your self-esteem and differentiates you from the procrastinators—that is, the type of procrastination that cripples effectiveness and goal achievement. An "all in one place" time organizer may be just the tool you've been looking for to help you to keep your promises and commitments.

Problem: Procrastination

Getting ready to get ready. As Mark Twain said, "Never put off until tomorrow what you can put off until the day after tomorrow." One of my Southern clients is always saying, "I'm fixin tuh." As soon as I hear that, I know he's telling me he won't be doing what he said he would be doing.

Solutions:

1. Get #1 done first! As you can see, many of these techniques are applicable to more than one time management challenge, just as the different time management situations are connected. One influences another. One bad habit can spill into and create another bad habit. But don't despair. One good habit also influences and creates other good habits. Ah, the legendary battle of the good guys versus the bad guys. Good always wins out, doesn't it? At least, as I believe, and in the movies, good always wins out in the long run.

2. Prioritize your goals. Surprise. This solution is part of the "Reasons Why" approach. The clearer you are on **What's In It For You**, the more powerful your resolve and commitment to moving forward, to taking action. To put it another way, if you have a big enough why, you'll figure out the how.

3. Set deadlines. Check your progress against deadlines. Without a deadline a goal remains a wish, a fantasy. Get your coach involved, especially when you're procrastinating and need that extra kick in the pants to get and keep going.

4. Don't leave jobs until the last minute. Some of us put things off until the last minute because of the pull of the trivial many, the habit of doing the easy first, of postponing the difficult. Doing the more difficult, the top priority tasks first is also a habit. I know this from my own experience. Several years ago I read about advice to complete tasks, to start with the more difficult ones first.

The question was asked, "How do you eat an elephant?" Answer: "One bite at a time." The lesson is that the best way to handle huge, important tasks is to break them down into smaller, more manageable parts. Also called "The Swiss Cheese Approach." It works. Slowly but surely, at least slowly for me, you start to develop these higher habits of completing tasks, beginning with the tougher tasks first. It definitely helps you feel better about yourself. As with everything, it's a process. A process that's moving you in the right direction, a direction that you have consciously chosen for yourself. A direction that leads you towards greater and greater personal and professional success.

Remember, we're all procrastinators. So no whipping of yourself for these bad habits. Hey, I just experienced some nice synchronicity. As I was writing this section I got a phone call from one of my coaches. He said that a TV morning show had just had on a guest discussing her new book, *It's About Time*. He said it was all about why people procrastinate and about the different time management types. Sounds like a book worth reading. He didn't catch the author's name.

Dr. Rob Gilbert, a sports psychologist at Montclair State University in New Jersey, and a friend of mine, recommends that going public with something helps you to overcome procrastination. He says, "Make a commitment, make it public, and know that I'll be back." Make your commitment public so that you'll be motivated to do what you said you were going to do. This helps you avoid the public humiliation of people knowing that you didn't keep your commitment. And once again, use the power of the coach, the power of the "I'll be back" Schwarzenegger Effect.

Another technique that Dr. Gilbert has had a lot of success with is in using the "avoidance of pain principle." He'll ask his client if there are any goals that they have set for themselves that are "non-negotiable," meaning that they **must** keep this commitment because it's an important goal, one that when accomplished will bring them great satisfaction, momentum, and pleasure. They want and choose to set this goal, but day after day, month after month, they keep putting off taking action.

Here's what Dr. Gilbert will have them do. If they don't take action, they have to pay someone a significant amount of money. For example, one of his clients kept on putting off starting a diet, starting to eat healthier foods. So, this is what he had her do. He asked her to give him a $500.00 check made out to her ex-husband. Now, she also gave him a stamped envelope addressed to the ex. He told her that if she didn't start her diet by the next Friday, he would put the envelope in the mail. Needless to say, she started the diet immediately. Dr. Gilbert also used other techniques of a similar nature to keep her on the diet. It all spelled success for her. This technique also works well in giving money to secretaries, coaches, friends, family members. If you don't keep your commitment, you have to give them money. It works with smaller amounts of money as well, but I suggest at least $100.00. The fear and pain of possibly losing the money will motivate you to take action.

Zig Ziglar, a well known motivational speaker and sales trainer, puts it another way. He says to go public with your "give up" goals, and to keep private your "go up" goals. The give up goals would be giving up smoking, drinking, weight, some bad habits. By going public this will motivate you to keep your commitment. Go up goals would be self-improvement goals, increase in sales goals, winning award goals, goals that if made public run the risk of getting some people jealous, which would lead to their lack of support, or at worst, possibly trying to undermine your success. Keeping them private means sharing them only with your coach, those in a position to help you achieve your goal, or other goal setters whose encouragement you know you will get. Sounds like good advice to me.

Having the habit of putting things off to the last minute brings us to the next time management challenge.

Problem: Crisis Management/Fire Fighting

Caused by procrastination, overreacting and failure to anticipate problems. Plus, failure to develop contingency plans. Crisis seems, based on thousands of years of people's experience, to be a part of life. What we need to do is minimize it. Left to its own devices, it can become too large a part of our life and become overwhelming.

Research indicates that a good time manager will spend 20-25 percent of his time dealing with crisis, whereas a poor time manager will spend 25-30 percent of his time. As you can see, the spread between a good time manager and a poor time manager can be anywhere from 0-50 percent (comparing 20 percent to 30 percent).

But either way, crisis management is a part of life. Every good manager that I have ever met, is good if not excellent at handling, and resolving a crisis. But, the truly great ones know how to minimize them.

Solutions:

1. Expect the unexpected. As we've learned from Murphy's Law: Whatever can go wrong, will go wrong, at the worst possible time, and cost you the most money.

2. Develop plans to prevent or limit consequences. Most of the crises that we face, are the same ones over and over again. Most of them are not total surprises. With that in mind, put together a plan. Plan out step-by-step what you will do the next time the reoccurring crisis happens. Of course, each crisis has its own style and flavor, but again, let's not throw the baby out with the bath water. These contingency plans can give us enough insight into the crisis, then we can tailor and flex the plans a bit, and this in turn allows us to effectively think on our feet. "An ounce of prevention . . . " as the saying goes. Failing forward, and learning from our mistakes.

3. Limit your response by

   a) Ignoring problems that can be ignored. Don't treat everything as if it's an "A1" priority. Everything is not a top priority. If you treat everything that way, you will drive yourself, and most of the people around you crazy.

   b) Delegating what others can handle. Make a "To Delegate" list. When I coach people on goal setting, too often I'll see goals like, "Be better organized," "Manage my time better," "Delegate more." Certainly, desirable aspirations, but as we've learned, it's not specific enough. How will you know when you're organized, managing time better, or delegating more? As we said before, "What gets measured gets managed." Without being able to measure your results, you'll have a tough time managing your progress, or fine-tuning your action plans, if you're getting off course.

   Here's a very effective and easy approach. Ask yourself, what will you be doing, when you're excellent at delegating. What will your coach see you doing that you're not currently doing. What will it look like to be great at delegating. Of course, write this all down, getting it specific and measurable. Now, you're on the path of learning how to effectively delegate. Then on your "To Delegate" list write out all of the opportunities that you have to delegate, and to whom.

    c) Handle only those crises which you alone can take care of. You don't have to get yourself involved in every crisis. As they say, "Pick your battles."

4. Recognize the dangers, the added pressure of procrastinating.

— Deadline pressure

— Impaired judgment under stress, which reminds me of our next solution.

5. Stop thinking that you "Work best under pressure," or that "You can do it better and faster yourself." The first one is an excuse, and the second one is the truth, at least for a while. The first statement is more of a habit than a reality. You may be one of those who have gotten into the habit of working under pressure, so this is the only way you have learned to work. Imagine how much better you might be, if you gave yourself the luxury of time to think and plan. My instincts tell me that you would probably still do some of your best thinking towards the end of the project, let's say the last 20 percent. But now, you've given yourself enough time to have done your homework, fine-tuned a few different options, and then really squeezed the best of the best ideas out of yourself.

I said that the second statement is true for a while, because if you do have this belief, that you can do it better yourself, in a very short period of time, that is exactly what will happen, you will be doing it all by yourself. Including the stress of having too much to do. You're a top achiever, so sure you can do it better than most people. But by not delegating you don't let the people around you grow, and you don't allow yourself to grow into more meaningful projects, since you're so taken up by all the little things that are still gripping your attention.

A simple rule of thumb is that if you know somebody who can do it 70 percent as well as you, have them do it. Give up on perfectionism. For most situations, outside of health issues, perfectionism is not required. Sometimes good is good enough. Again, choose your battles. The person who is currently doing it at 70 percent of your capacity, will in due time get close, if not better to your ability. Give them the opportunity to grow through delegation. Delegation is not dumping responsibility on people. It's about explaining projects, and monitoring their progress. Delegation gets the job done, and it motivates growth.

6. Stop getting off on being "The Hero!" I worked for a guy for several years that loved creating a crisis. He would purposefully change direction at the drop of a hat midstream. He loved that people had to come to him for his expertise in order to "right the ship." He loved the excitement of things getting out of control, and then, as he saw it, because of his quick response and decisiveness he was able to save the day. Of course he nearly drove everybody around him crazy.

This is part of a time management style. Some people love it when things get hectic, and the adrenaline gets pumping. They thrive on the high stimulation. Their excitement quotient is sky high. This probably won't change, it's a part of who they are. Not a problem . . . for them. Recognize it as a valid time management style, but make sure that you don't force it on others needlessly. If you trigger this "fire alarm" response in those around you too often, who don't share this style, eventually it will wear them down, stress them out, and they'll start to resent your style, and resist your leadership.

Problem: Telephone/Voice Mail/E-Mail Interruptions

Caused by having no plan for making or taking calls, an inability to terminate conversations, and ineffective screening of calls, voice mail and e-mail.

Solutions:

1. Develop a plan to screen calls. If you have an assistant, get him or her involved. Your assistant's responsibility is not to keep everybody away from you. Their job is to keep the people who are going to waste your time, away from you. Put together a "blessed or pest" list to give them the proper guidelines on who you want to speak to, and who not.

   It might go something like this, "Hold all of my calls for the next hour, except if Tom Willings or Laura Bowman call." Use common sense and balance here. Balance meaning, it may not be wise to screen out all salespeople. It's important to keep informed of the leading edge changes going on all around us, and a knowledgeable, professional salesperson is someone who can help keep us informed. Also balance in terms of your own "druthers." Tailor this screening to your own situation, but it is something that I urge you to consider. Even if you answer your own phone, you can use an answering machine, or voice mail to screen out calls, during those times that you're in your office, and need to have times of silence without interruption, in order to think more effectively.

2. Using the power of the quiet hour. Typically this technique is known for being an hour, but it certainly can be just as effective being a quiet 1/2 hour, a quiet 15 minutes. As you're doing your daily priority list at the end of the day, think your next day out, and schedule in times for taking calls, and for making calls. The times you choose are of course flexible, as your day changes as you get into it. I don't recommend that you always take calls just as they come in. As we discussed before, most of what we do is not split second, must take action now type situations.

   You can still take calls as they come in for most of the day, but as you look at your daily priority list, and see important projects that are going to need your undivided attention, this is where you schedule times to group the calls that you make and take. Add this with a good screening system, and you'll be better at getting that necessary quiet time. Alec Mackenzie, in his great book, *The Time Trap*, waxes eloquent, and in much further detail than here, on the power of the quiet hour.

3. Learn how to end phone calls. For some folks this is a biggee. I know, and you probably know as well, people who just can't seem to end a phone conversation. These might be people that you're talking to for the first time, but it's usually with people that you talk with every once in a while. You know from past experience, that if this call is to end, you'll have to be the one ending it. Not that they ramble on, which sometimes they do, but it just seems that they cannot bring themselves to make a statement that signals that it's time to finish the call. Some lack of confidence and assertiveness, yes, with a little bit of, I don't want to appear rude, mixed in.

   If you have this problem, and it can be a problem, you'll be making your phone calls 40-50 percent longer than they need to be, which will waste up to an hour or more a day of your precious time, based on the volume of calls that you make or take.

   Here's what to do: 1) Present a time limit to the call, "Yes, I can talk for five minutes," or when you're making the call, "Terry, what we have to talk about will just take a few minutes." 2) Announce the ending of the call, "Kate, before we hang up . . . " and, 3) Be candid, "Sorry John, I have to go now." All a part of our time management philosophy of being ruthless with time, but gracious with people.

4. Attitude adjustment. Have the attitude that it's your job calling. Can you imagine going into your office, and hearing the good news? "The phones have stopped ringing!" The bad news would soon follow, "We're out of business." The telephone is an under utilized high tech piece of equipment. With all of the exciting technological breakthroughs, the telephone has started to be taken for granted. It is still one of our most powerful business weapons. These simple and effective techniques will help us to use it more effectively.

A quick word on voice mail and e-mail. Also great business tools when used properly. Unfortunately, too many people abuse their use, resulting in them becoming one more time management burden instead of a technological tool designed to improve the quality of our lives. I read an article recently where a Chief Financial Officer of a top 100 company went on vacation for a week to come back to over 2,000 e-mails. He just pressed delete, figuring if they were important enough messages, he would hear from them again.

Recently I have had more of my clients asking for advice concerning voice and e-mail. My advice is similar to the making/taking calls advice, plus one additional pointer. If you want, when the work flow, or concentration flow allows, just answer them as they come in. But when you need those times of silence and deep thought, schedule times for taking the messages and then schedule in time for making calls and responding to e-mail. I know a lot of managers now, who effectively use these new message technologies effectively . . . meaning they get their messages out, and save time in the process.

The one additional piece of advice. As an assistant/supervisor, small team, department, or company you need to set up systems, procedures within the culture that respect the time of each individual. Make a conscious effort not to abuse these technologies. Common sense, as always, can bring us a long way. We don't need to be leaving messages for everything, and we certainly don't need to be leaving messages to cover ourselves, to say, "Hey, I left you a message," or to be used as personnel documentation. If this becomes part of the culture, with big or small groups, people are leaving messages for everybody, and time gets abused. Use your common sense and let people know when they should be leaving messages. Give them company guidelines on how to effectively use voice and e-mail.

Problem: Drop-In Visitors

Caused by the desire to always be available, an open-door policy, and no plan for handling interruptions.

Solutions:

1. Arrange appointments with those people that you need to see on a regular basis. This way, aside from emergencies, they can hold off some discussions until they see you at the regularly scheduled meeting. How often to schedule these types of meetings is your, and your people's call.

I believe that **people treat you the way you train them to treat you**. If you let them know that it's OK to just come walking into your office at any time, that's what they will do. Again, common sense rules. Yes, there are times that it is appropriate, and effective, for people to be just dropping in, but there are also other times when people swarming in on you is not effective. Develop the culture that works best for you, but have some kind of system that your people understand, so they clearly know what is expected.

2. Redefine "open" to mean "accessible." Open and accessible to those who need assistance, when they need your help.
3. Have a quiet time with your door closed. Let those people who need to, know how long your door will be closed. Let them know why you're closing your door, if you feel that this added information will help them to be more effective in guarding your quiet time. Knowing the importance of the project you're working on, will motivate most people to honor your request of not being disturbed.

   In some company cultures it's an unwritten law that no one ever closes their door. So, do what you must do, to be "politically correct," but you can still institute quiet time even with your door open, by following some of the above guidelines. If you don't have a door, find a hideaway, an isolated spot in the office, letting those people who need to, know where you are. These next two techniques work well for those with, or without a door.
4. Go to the offices of others. It's easier for you to leave other people's offices, than it is for you to get them to leave yours.
5. Develop subtle techniques. When they do come into your office, stand up when they enter. This will signal to them that you're busy, and don't have a lot of time for idle chit chat. Start walking them towards the door if they don't get the hint.

Problem: Attempting Too Much

I've had some managers smile when I say this is a time management problem. They love it when they hear that their people are attempting too much ... they feel that this is a nice problem to have. To a certain degree I agree. It's not so easy finding good, hard working, committed, loyal, motivated employees. So, I see their point. But, don't smile too deeply. You don't want attempting too much, to turn out to really be just a bunch of out-of-focus chickens running around with their heads cut off, turning into burn-out, and low productivity.

Attempting too much is caused by not separating the urgent (something that begs for your immediate attention) from the important (something that moves you towards your relevant, high impact goals). In *The 7 Habits of Highly Effective People* Stephen Covey does a masterful job of explaining how to separate the urgent from the important. He explains it very simply, and powerfully by using a quadrant. Recommended reading, if not must reading. Attempting too much is also caused by not setting priorities or by not planning.

Solutions:

1. Set daily, weekly, monthly, and yearly goals. My passion, and hopefully soon to be yours. Well, if not a passion, at least a disciplined, easy for you to do habit.

2. Focus on top priorities. Back to our time management philosophy: There is never enough time for everything, but there is always enough time for the most important thing. The vital few versus the trivial many. Major in majors.

3. Take 5-10 minutes at the end of each day to plan for the next day. Everybody knows about this daily priority list technique, very few implement it on a consistent basis. Do or do not, there is no try.

4. Say, "No" when appropriate. There are several self-help books exclusively covering this one topic . . . having difficulty saying no to people. It seems to have something to do with wanting to be liked. Saying no graciously and effectively is a four-step process:

    A) Listen. Really hear and understand what is being asked of you.

    B) Say, "No."

    C) Give reasons

    D) Suggest alternatives.

    It comes down to this—**if you're not clear on your priorities, other people's priorities will become your priorities.** When you are clear on your priorities, you will more effectively say no. For example, "No John, I won't be able to review that report with you now. I have a 3 PM deadline on this project. Perhaps we can meet for breakfast tomorrow." If you feel that saying "No" is too direct or too harsh, you can cushion the "No" by saying, "John, normally I would jump at the chance to help you with that report, but I have a 3 PM deadline that must be met. Perhaps we can meet for breakfast tomorrow, or Susan, who is familiar with that report, might be in a better position to help you." Note: Learning how to tactfully and skillfully say "No" helps with calendar clutter.

    If it's your boss that's asking you to do something, here's how you would handle it: "Right now I'm working on the XYZ account, what you're asking me to do, is it more important than what I'm currently working on?" Your boss might say yes it is more important, in which case you would stop what you're working on, and begin on the higher priority, or your boss might say no, keep on working on what your working on. Clear priorities give you more control over your life. Working on your relevant, doing what counts, high impact activities.

If you have multiple bosses (2 or more) who all come to you, within a short period of time, each with their own A1, top, do it right now priority, call a **Time Out**. Explain to them what just happened, that you're one person, and that you need further guidance from them. Sort it out amongst themselves, which priority you'll do first, second and so forth. This works! Manage your bosses well. Train them, break them in right.

5. Delegate more when possible. Take my advice from before. Put together a very specific "To Delegate" list, and then implement it.

More Techniques With A Little Advice Mixed In

1. Accept the fact that **you** are the cause of many of your time management problems. Don't be blaming others. Figure out what you're going to do about it.

2. Your number one time saver still remains that all time favorite: Thinking in advance and planning . . . setting those goals! Plan your day with these three giants in mind: What are my goals? What are my priorities? What does my ideal day look like? Then **write it down**! in the form of a daily priority list. Nothing is more powerful than a written plan with deadlines.

3. If you still haven't gotten this message, let me come at it one more time. **What gets written gets done!!!** Put your ego aside, you know the ego that's thinking, "I don't need to write things down, that's for people of lesser talents."

   Stop relying on your memory. When you see me writing something down, 99.99 percent of the time it gets done, and done within the agreed upon time frame.

4. Expect delays and interruptions. Build in safety cushions. If you expect something to take 45 minutes, schedule an hour.

5. Show up on time. In fact, plan to be 10 minutes early. This is very professional, and considerate of others, which they definitely appreciate, and take positive notice of.

6. Fallacy: The more meetings you attend, the more important you are.

   Reality: Most meetings are too long, and waste too much time of too many people. A lot of them should not be held at all.

Some simple guidelines:
- Start on time.
- No meeting without a purpose. Have clear written goals and objectives for all meetings.
- No meeting without a written agenda.
- Time frames for each topic. This will keep you and the group focused and on track.
- End on time.

7. Have a "Things to Read" folder. Scan, tear, skim, highlight, and underline. Be in the habit of reading with a highlighter, or a pen handy. When you go back to read that all important book/article, instead of it taking you a couple of days/weeks to reread, it'll take you a couple of hours to refresh your memory on the key points.

   Instead of having a depressing pile (I meet a lot of people who suffer from piles) of magazines stacked away in some corner of your office, just look at the table of contents, and circle those articles you want to read. Then either yourself or your assistant can tear them out and put them into this folder. Take the folder with you when traveling. You'll be caught up with your "must" reading in no time. Probably not getting to all the reading you would love to, but definitely caught up with the most important articles/books in your life.

8. Know your "Prime Time." The time of day when your energy and mental clarity is at its highest. For me, I'm consistently at my prime during the morning hours. Many a time, I'll be struggling with something late in the afternoon, or early evening. I know to put it aside, which 90 percent of the time I can, since I have allowed enough cushion of time, and I'm not jamming everything into the last minute. I'll put it aside for the morning, and sure enough, what was a struggle the night before, is a breeze in the morning. Know thyself. Know when you're predictably, and consistently at your best.

   Use this time to do your most important/productive work. Coordinate this prime time with your quiet time when you can. It makes for a very powerful combination.

ANOTHER K.I.S.S. FROM ME

A quick review, plus a little additional fine-tuning on some previously discussed ideas.

The Most Common Techniques to Get & Stay Organized . . . the Five Major Parts

1. An organized desk.
2. A file system (I haven't mentioned this yet).
   — Aside from the necessary client/topic folders you'll need four color coded folders marked:
     - Urgent
     - Daily Priorities
     - Phone Calls/Voice Mail
     - Correspondence/Dictation/E-Mail
3. Sort your paperwork, and placed by you or your assistant in the proper folder. Some papers will go in permanent folders, others in one of the above four folders. Coordinate this with your planning of the next day.
4. Use a time organizer (paper or electronic) on a daily basis. Don't get hung-up if you're not using it exactly the way you were instructed. Yes, I have heard fabulous success stories about how time organizers how been the key to some people's success. How the organizer helped them get focused and finally organized, leading to achieving more of their goals. I don't doubt these testimonials. But, don't whip yourself for not using the organizer 100 percent the way you were told. Adapt it to your own needs. I did.
5. Handle paperwork only once.

These are the **Big 5**. Using these will get you 80 percent + towards being a great time manager.

Ah, That Clutter Thing Again

This is for the truly ambitious, or the truly neurotic, depending upon your point of view. Obviously I allow for different styles, recognizing that there is no one right way. Some people respond to the following guidelines with great results. Others, are thinking, give me a break. This book welcomes both opinions.

Our goal here is not to clean up your work space. Our goal is to get and **keep** you uncluttered. Too often a client of mine will call me up urging me to come right over to see their beautifully clean, organized, uncluttered office. I'll tell them I'll be over in a few days. They say no I must come over right now. They're saying this because they know that when I come over in a few days the mess will be back. So, who's fooling who? That's the goal, to get and stay uncluttered.

A Step-by-Step Procedure to Get Uncluttered

Supplies: A letter or legal-sized pad
100 file folders, 1/3 each of left, center, and right tabs
3-5 expandable file pockets, size 3 1/2"

1. You'll need about **two hours of uninterrupted time** to organize your desk, get rid of all those piles, and file papers you want to keep.
2. Schedule an appointment with yourself. Write it on your calendar and keep the appointment.
3. Close the door, turn off the phone, and allow no interruptions.
4. **Bring a dumpster!**
5. The whole process begins with the top of your desk.
6. Go through every paper in each pile and separate the papers you need to keep from the papers that can be thrown away.
7. Pick up a piece of paper and look at it. If there's any work that needs to be done or action that needs to be taken, keep it. Start a pile of papers to keep. If you don't need it, **throw it away**!
8. Go through all the papers you kept and make a *Daily Priority List*, a list of unfinished work and ongoing projects.
9. Start with the paper on the top and ask yourself, "Is there any work to be done?" If yes, write it on your daily priority list.
10. Do you now need to keep this paper? If no, throw. If yes, file. File in a properly labeled file. Master filing will be discussed in step 12. For now, put it aside to be filed.
11. Now, go through all the papers one by one.
12. Create Master Files—Find a place for the papers you keep.
    - Use new file folders. Rule: Never put a piece of *unfinished work* inside a file folder without noting it on your daily priority list. Step 16 covers what you do with your completed daily priority list. If it isn't written on the list, it will be forgotten.
    - Have tabs in three (3) separate positions, left, center, right and stagger them. This saves time since you can now see three file labels at once, which makes it easier to locate.
    - Write file labels by hand. Write with a pen directly on the tab. This saves time.
    - Place each group of related papers in a file folder.
    - You'll need a generic file, it can be titled, "Relevant/Important." Some papers will go in one of the four color coded folders mentioned before. Once work in these files are completed, place the paper in a permanent file or throw out.

- Keep a supply of unused file folders in your desk drawer.
- As an option to pendaflex (hanging) folders, you can use 3 1/2" expandable file pockets placed inside your file drawers. They take up less space, are more affordable, and its different, which makes them fun to use. Also look for expandable files numbered 1-31, and January-December. If you can't find them, use the standard pendaflex files.
- Your most important files are placed in the file drawer in your desk. The rest in a credenza or a filing cabinet.
- File related folders together in file pockets.
- Arrange folders in order of importance or according to frequency used, not alphabetically.
- Clean out the file drawer in your desk. The file drawer inside your desk is the most important drawer in your office. Use it to store your most important papers and files.
- As necessary remove hanging file folders to make room for your expandable file pockets.

13. The next step is to organize the papers from any old files. Some of them can be merged with the new files. Some need to be thrown out. This will be done over time. This is not part of your two hour meeting with yourself.

14. An efficient desk is easy to maintain.

- Decide *immediately* which papers to toss and which to keep.
- File paper *immediately* in the appropriate file or create a new file.

    Note: Make a *habit* of *immediately*. It you don't do it immediately the piles come back very quickly. So, no procrastination here. The split seconds that it takes you to put it away now, save you moments and minutes later, plus it raises self-esteem, and minimizes regret and guilt.

- Tips to stay organized:

    — always note on a daily priority list or put into your "Relevant/Important" file any unfinished work or future projects.

    — pull files when you need them and put them away *immediately*.

    — when you see piles accumulating, which during the course of a perfectly normal day will happen several times a day, stop cold and reorganize yourself. You'll do it a few times a day, and it will only take a couple of minutes to get yourself back together. So, don't despair when you see the piles piling up. It's just reality reminding you to take a moment to get it back together.

15. Now, open your door and feel good about yourself, and what you have just achieved! Sit back in your chair, put your feet up on your clean desk, take a deep comforting breath, and relax. All you can see on your desk is your telephone and your daily priority list. That's all.

16. How to use your daily priority list. We've mentioned most of these, but here's an "all in one place" reminder, with a few additional points.

    — last thing that you look at before you leave the office in the evening, and the first thing your review when you arrive in the morning.

    — if you're using a time organizer, fine, if not, a simple lined pad of paper, letter or legal, will do just fine. I recommend staying away from small pieces of paper. They can quickly pile up, and can be easily lost, adding to clutter and confusion.

    — write on every line. Get into the habit of writing everything down.

    — don't rewrite your list everyday.

    — draw a line through finished work. This feels so good. Cross off as you transfer from old list to new list.

    — make a new list when the old list is starting to get too cumbersome. This is usually every 1-2 weeks.

    — date your list.

    — keep a folder titled, "Old Lists." Along with keeping your monthly goal sheets, these make for excellent journals to look back on, and to see your progress.

    — use a pen. Pencil, in a few short days, starts to get too messy. Also, written in pencil, old lists can make for poor journals, since the writing may become illegible. Pencil works OK in daily planners.

    — keep your daily priority list on top of your desk. All you have on your desk is your telephone, your daily priority list, and the thing that you're working on. Several times a day you just get reorganized.

    You may also decide to keep your monthly goals on your desk, as a constant reminder of where you have decided to focus your attention. Or, your monthly goals may be kept in a drawer that you open up often or enlarged and posted on a wall where you will see them.

Here are different benefits people tell me they get from using a daily priority list:

- more in control
- for my own inner peace/calm

- I feel less horrible, less of that unfocused feeling
- sleep better
- enjoy my evenings more
- start the day with tremendous momentum
- know at the end of the day what I have accomplished
- achieve more of my goals

Knowledge Is Potential Power, The Time Management Contract

Now you know it, now you do it. Where to begin? I had asked you to circle the techniques that you felt would be of most benefit to you. Here's why.

1. Look again at your top five time wasters.
2. Look at all of the techniques that you circled.
3. Pick out the three that you believe will help you the most.

Now, make a commitment in writing.

Time Management Contract

I agree to commit to using, over the next four weeks, the three following time management strategies to improve my efficiency and effectiveness.

-

-

-

I will report my results to _____ during the week of _____ .

Name   Date

Once you have mastered, or have made progress on these three techniques, pick out another three, and then another three. It's best to start with a small core group. Three at a time keeps you focused, and is manageable to measure your progress.

Enjoy your results!

Chapter Ten

Looking for a Few Good Managers— The Big Squeeze

It all starts with desire, and the attitude, "Hey, give it a chance." When you give it a chance, the results will be there for you . . . guaranteed. I also guarantee the results will not be there, if you don't give it a chance, if you don't use this material.

When you give it a chance, over the months your goals get S.M.A.R.T.er and S.M.A.R.T.er, and with it your daily planning becomes more and more powerful. You know what to do, and you do it. Your coach is right there to help you constantly fine-tune your approach, which speeds up the learning process.

The Goal Achievement Process (G.A.P.) **squeezes** out your potential, as well as the excuses. When you meet with your coach/manager on a regular monthly basis, to review your past months results, it helps squeeze out the right course of action that you need to take, as you review what's working, and what's not working. It allows your coach/manager to be on top of things that you're working on, so you can have the full benefit of their support and additional suggestions/insights. I've seen it happen over and over again. It definitely squeezes out the potential of the coach/manager as well.

If you're out of focus, unsure of what to do, unclear of what direction to take, this process squeezes out your frustrations. Sometimes when we're frustrated, because of some old bad habits, we try to cover our assets, by making all of these nonsense excuses. This activates the "B.S. Meter" in your coach's mind. But this can be a positive as well. It gives your coach/manager a chance to hear the nonsense, and to quickly nip it in the bud. Again, I have heard it all, as I have sat in on coaching sessions.

Because we haven't hit our goals, we tend to get defensive, and this is when the blaming or excuse making flourishes. A great coach will be able to point out the B.S. Most people know it when they hear it themselves, and with their coaches/managers help start to self-correct. The excuses fade away. Action planning, and action doing, soon become the dominant theme. Desired results are achieved.

Add, Delete, Fine-Tune

Three simple words for a coach to use as a guideline in the one-to-one monthly coaching sessions. When looking at someone's monthly goals, or daily planning, always be looking for what you have to add, delete, or fine-tune. What goals do they need to add? What goals do they need to delete, to drop off from this months list? What goals need to be re-prioritized, or fine-tuned? Fine-tuned meaning getting them S.M.A.R.T.

Ideally the manager and the coach are one and the same person. Sometimes the manager is a poor coach. Then it becomes the blind leading the blind. If this is the case, use my previous suggestion of finding a coach amongst your peers, or in your industry, or from someone whose advice you respect. These three easy pieces of the coaching process will help a manager to become a better coach.

Peer Group Review Associations

We don't coach everybody the same. We give them what they need ... whatever it takes ... to get the desired results. Closing the gap between where they are, and where they want to be.

Some of your people you'll be meeting with on a regular monthly basis. Intensive, constructive one-on-one's until both of you are sure that everything's on track. Clear that the necessary skills and habits are developing. Some of your people you'll need to meet with, only on a quarterly basis, for the one-on-one review. Making sure that no bad habits are forming, and making sure that they know that you're there for them when they need you.

Others are off and running on their own. That is with regards to goal setting being a habit, and getting results. I suggest that these people get together with their peers on a monthly, or quarterly basis, without the coach there. Coach can be there if invited. Help coach each other. Keep lively that invaluable process of sharing ideas. The ideal group size is 4-7 people. Each person gets to read their goals out loud to the group, and gets the benefit of everybody's feedback. Set a time limit of two hours to give everybody a chance to review their progress.

Whatever the scenario, definitely keep everybody in the habit of setting goals every month, during the 6 day window. Have everybody give/mail/fax to you their monthly goals, by the third day into the new month. Look over their goals and get back to them with any of your additions, deletions, or fine-tuning recommendations.

That's it.

Managing Multiple Priorities— Doing More With Less

I get asked about these two topics quite often. Because of all of the downsizing/rightsizing in companies, more is expected from the people who stay with the company. Everything that we have talked about up to this point **is about these two topics**. When you're clear on your goals. When both you and your manager agree on your key result areas, your high impact, doing what counts activities. When you put the 80/20 rule to work for you, what you are doing is managing multiple priorities, and learning how to do more with less. Less in this case, meaning less people doing more work.

Sometimes when people ask about managing multiple priorities, they're asking if I know of any software, any formats to help them track the progress of their different top priority projects. My answer is yes and no.

Yes, there is software of this kind available, no there is no one format that I recommend over any other. Especially be careful of the formats that do meet your needs, but are not simple to use. In fact, that is one of my goals. To put all of my material, with all of the necessary bells and whistles, and screen savers, onto one easy to use, K.I.S.S. software package. I'm currently negotiating with several companies to develop this software.

Yes, there are formats that you can now use. A daily priority list, setting monthly goals, review sessions with your coach, and using an all in one place time organizer. These will definitely help you to manage multiple priorities, and do more with less.

Parkinson's Law: Work will expand to fill the time available. The "right" rightsizing of a company has the potential to draw more potential out of its people. Effectively using the time available to them, in a focused, disciplined, exciting, productive manner.

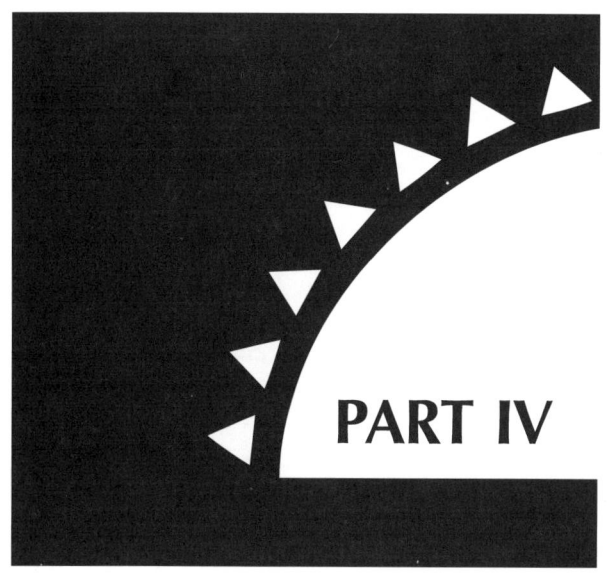

PART IV

The Next Step

CHAPTER ELEVEN

The Mystical Side of Goal Setting

"Until one is committed, there is hesitancy, the chance to draw back, always ineffectiveness, concerning all acts of initiative and creation.

There is one elementary truth the ignorance of which kills countless ideas and splendid plans; **that the moment one definitely commits oneself, then providence moves too. All sorts of things occur to help one that would never otherwise have occurred.** *A whole stream of events issues from the decision, raising in one's favor all manner of unforeseen incidents and meetings and material assistance which no man could have dreamed would have come his way.*

Whatever you can do or dream you can do, begin it. Boldness has genius, power and magic in it. Begin it now!"

—Goethe

When you're in the zone, the above definitely happens. Interesting that when an athlete is in the zone they say, "I was unconscious." Unconscious meaning, he or she could do no wrong. Everything was happening spontaneously and effortlessly. Peak performance was no longer a theory, a quest, it was being realized. Goal setting and putting into action your plans, are two things that can trigger the zone. That plus patience and innocence. You cannot force or will it to happen, you can only set up the proper circumstances through your focus, commitment and practice to maximize the opportunity/chance that it can happen. Then, it's thy will be done. With this in mind, here are four stories. Three are from people I coached. One is from someone I met.

One of My Favorite Goal Achievement Success Stories: 6:11

I was working with Paul. One of his goals was simply written as **6:11**. I asked him what it meant. He explained that every morning before he left for work, he and his wife would set a goal for what train he would catch to come home. He realized he was spending too much time at work and not enough time with his family. **6:11** would give him more balance and enjoyment. From this one simple goal, which profoundly meets all of the criteria of a S.M.A.R.T. goal, Paul realized three distinct benefits/results:

1. Ninety percent of the time he caught the **6:11**. Result: More time with family!

2. Paul would now get to his top daily priorities earlier in the day. No longer did he leave things for the last moment. This helped him cut back on procrastinating and helped him develop the habit of getting to his top, most important priorities first. Result: His days are now more productive.

3. Remember when I talked about the philosophy **"People treat you the way you train them to treat you"**? Paul told his staff that everyday he was catching the **6:11**. He told them to come to him for help earlier in the day. They would have to break the habit of coming to him at the last moment. This caused a crisis management mode forcing him to leave work later and later. Result: His people became focused on their daily priorities and developed a new habit of getting to him earlier. The whole team was now more focused and more productive. Paul was no longer the beneficiary of their poor planning.

This one simple, yet profound goal is helping Paul and his team achieve what I tell my audiences/clients is the real challenge of success: Not only to be successful but to **enjoy** your success.

Controlling College Expenses While Teaching Your Child About Money

I met John at a party and he told me about this great system he had successfully implemented with his daughter Lynn, when she went off to college.

This system meets all the criteria of S.M.A.R.T. goals and for being proactive, meaning planning this **before** she went off to college. John's goal: To manage college expenses **and** to give his child the skills to be able to manage her own finances when she graduates. Note: At first this was John's goal. Over time and with his parenting, coaching, it became both of their goal. Right from the beginning, John treated Lynn as an equal partner in setting and implementing the plan.

Here are some of the main components of John and Lynn's system:

- Set up two separate bank accounts, each with a debit card. One for parent responsible expenses (Account A), and one for student responsible expenses (Account B).

- Identify fair amounts, negotiated between parent and child, for expenditures. Parent does not micro-manage, track how the money is spent.

- Account A is set up by the parent. Parent puts in starter money. Statement to parent.

- The agreed upon monthly amount is deposited via check into Account B, which is set up by student. Statement to student. In addition to parents money amount, student puts own money into account.

Clearly define who is responsible for what expenses. Sample:

Parent	Student
Phone calls home	All other calls
Travel to/from home	All other travel
Medical expenses	Phone calls from home
Monthly allowance	*Food

*Food spending is student's responsibility. Parent either pays board or monthly lump sum, but does not track spending.

Provide incentives, as in real life. If she calls three weeks into the month, and is out of money, don't bail her out. Let her learn the hard lessons. If at the end of the month she hasn't spent all of her money, she keeps it, while receiving her upcoming month's full allowance. Again, the parent doesn't track how the money or how much was spent.

John also made getting scholarship money a part of the arrangement. He shared 50/50 of the money up to $5,000 ($2,500 each, payable quarterly). This motivated Lynn to fill out the forms and keep up the grades. Also, costs after four years of college are the student's expense.

Sample Agreement:

Financial Arrangements for Lynn While at College

While Lynn is at college, here's how we'll handle various financial transactions:

> Mom/Dad will pay for tuition, room and board, and meal plans.
>
> Lynn will open a bank account at a local college bank in her name and Social Security number. It will have a checking account and a MAC card for withdrawing cash from cash machines.
>
> Lynn should use the VISA or MasterCard from New Jersey for items that Mom/Dad are responsible for.
>
> All cash that Lynn has earned from her working and from gifts shall be deposited into the college bank account and will be Lynn's full responsibility. Lynn can withdraw cash from this account via MAC card or by cashing a check. Any subsequent earnings would go directly into this account as well.
>
> Any shared scholarship money will be deposited into Lynn's college account in four equal payments spaced throughout the year, less any funds owed by Lynn to Mom/Dad.
>
> $ _____ per month will be deposited by Mom/Dad into the college bank account for miscellaneous spending money.
>
> All reasonable ground travel expenses between college and home will be reimbursed. Other travel will be reimbursed only at Mom/Dad's discretion.
>
> Telephone calls to home will be for Mom/Dad's account, all other telephone calls are Lynn's expense.
>
> Medical costs will be paid by Mom/Dad.
>
> _____   _____   _____
> Mom/Dad Signature   Lynn's Signature   Date

There were specific lessons that John wanted Lynn to learn. These are some of my favorite's:

- Money is finite. When you use it up, it's gone.
- A credit card is real money.
- A hundred little things add up to a lot of money.
- The real world doesn't care about your personal financial issues.

- Two credit cards is enough.
- Don't withdraw more than you need. If your self-control is weak you'll spend more.
- What you've saved, you've earned.

As mentioned, John set this up with Lynn before she started college. He never asked her what she specifically felt/thought about this arrangement. When she graduated in four years, John asked Lynn to send him an e-mail about her feelings on how they had arranged the finances. Here are some of the highlights from that letter:

- Overall, I feel our financial agreement has worked out well. It was fair.
- It was easy to keep track of, and prevented a lot of arguments.
- Helping me with my expenses allowed me to focus on my studies, and my Grade Point Average benefited.
- Two separate credit cards is a good idea. I appreciate your trust.
- Sharing scholarship funds was extremely kind on your part. Being smart in school paid off literally.
- I learned the value of money. I learned how to budget for the month. It wasn't always easy.
- I don't know if I would have done anything differently. All in all, this system was pretty great. Way to go Dad!

I was very impressed when John told me about this system. After reading the e-mail, I was equally impressed with Lynn. Obviously, someone who has her values in order. Someone who knows how fortunate she is have such great, caring parents.

The Other Two Stories

It was obvious to me how talented and competent David was. He really knew his stuff. Just as obvious was his high level of integrity towards his work and towards the people in his department.

When I first coach someone, I tell them that there isn't a lot of preparation for the first meeting. Just bring the goal setting exercises from the workshop, and their upcoming months goals, if they have already written them down.

David came to our first meeting with a lot of great ideas, but they were scattered all over the place. Meaning very few had time frames, and none were specific or measurable. While he was describing his goals to me, I got this very clear image of these goals being "on top of the shelf" goals. We could just about see the goals, but they were a little bit out of our reach. Out of our reach because they weren't S.M.A.R.T.

Within an hour we got all of David's goals S.M.A.R.T. As I always do I told him, "I'll be back," in a month. Two and a half weeks later I got a call from David. He said, "You wouldn't believe all of the positive changes that have happened to me since we last met." I had no problem believing them at all. When I first met him the potential was clearly there for great and exciting things to happen for him, all he needed was a coach to help him to get his goals specific and measurable, and then to assign time frames to them. We did, and he reaped the benefits.

Three months later he got some news that most people would call a major setback. His entire department was being downsized, actually made obsolete, since the company had decided to outsource his entire department. He wasn't needed any longer. He was out of a job.

He didn't panic. He told me he believed that this was for the best, that his goals really wouldn't change that much because of this. It just would be that he would have to accomplish them elsewhere. He was totally confident that that elsewhere would appear soon. He fine-tuned his goals a little, and then took the necessary action to find a better position within the same industry. You already know what I'm about to tell you. Yes, within two months David called me and said that he had landed his dream job. Now, his goals are reaching even higher.

One other thing that struck me about David was his innocence and his belief that things would work out for the best. It wasn't a mood, a pollyanna attitude that he was creating to fool or soothe himself, it was a solid "no doubt" belief. This plus the added advantage of clear goals keeps triggering the zone for him.

Kathy is very different from David, but you'll see similar results, a similar pattern.

Like so many other people she firmly believed that goals were important, but she had never written down a goal in her life. After my workshop she decided to take advantage of coaching. By our second meeting you could see that she was generating tremendous momentum for herself. She had set some very ambitious goals. All of her relevant goals were being exceeded. What she said next really caught my attention.

"I'm achieving goals from the past that I haven't even written down yet. Goals that I had thought about, but never made a full commitment to. You know they were my, "Wouldn't it be nice goals."

I'm also hitting some goals that I thought were much more than a stretch, they were just wishful thinking. For example, I never focused on getting a promotion, and when we had our first coaching session you helped me realize that I was feeling a little left out about not even being considered for the last few promotions that came up. So, we wrote down a specific promotion, and in the last month I have had three offers to consider."

Just as with David, where I got the image of "taking goals off of a shelf," with Kathy I got the image of a vortex. She had created a momentum that was bringing goals from all areas of her life into focus, and into being realized. She was experiencing the magic of goal setting. The quote from Goethe was not theory, she was living and enjoying it. Once she definitely made a commitment, this part of the quote was a reality, "all sorts or things occur to help one that would never otherwise have occurred. **A whole stream of events issues from the decision, raising in one's favor all manner of unforeseen incidents and meetings and material assistance which no one could have dreamed would have come her way.**"

I was fortunate to meet David and Kathy at the same time. Their experiences reminded me that every once in a while I meet people where goal setting is magical. They just get their goals S.M.A.R.T. and they're off and running. I haven't scientifically researched this, but my gut reaction is that this happens for about 1-5 percent of the people that I meet and coach. So I'm saying it happens for 1-5 percent of the 1-5 percent who write down their goals.

I'm not in that 1-5 percent of the 1-5 percent . . . at least not yet. The current patterns in my life show me more as a "slow and steady wins the race" kind of guy. You know, the tortoise and the hare story. I may not quite be a tortoise, but I definitely relate more to that side of the fable.

Hitting 30-40 percent of my goals the first few months that I had made a commitment to goal setting, then moving up to 50 percent for the next year or so. Getting my goals S.M.A.R.T.er and S.M.A.R.T.er, and moving into the 60-75 percent range during my 2nd and 3rd year. Finally in my 4th year moving beyond just monthly goal setting, and starting to get a vision for myself, my business, and my family. Starting to set goals 1-2-3-5-10-20 years out. Now, hitting the stride of achieving on a consistent basis 85-95 percent of what I wrote down. Having a clear vision and mission after 5 years of dedicated, habitual goal setting. As the gospel song tells it so well, "God Ain't Finished with Me Yet."

The Next Step

After five years of "easy does it" goal setting I had created a clear and specific mission for my life. "Easy does it" meaning, I just wrote down my goals every month. Not paying much attention to those little demons that kept whispering in my ear, "Stop fooling around, stop wasting your time writing down these stupid goals."

Here's why I'm calling this last section "the next step." It has to do with that 90-99 percent of our potential that we are not using. That part of your self that it is my mission to help you enliven. My goals have lead me to this mission.

It's common knowledge that we are not using our full potential. Ever wonder what lies within that 90-99 percent that we're not using? I think the reason that we all need and want to know the next step(s) in a process, is because we all know ... deep within ourselves ... that we ourselves are a process unfolding. We know that there is so much more to be realized, and actualized about our own potential. No matter how well we're doing in life, there is still a tremendous amount not being used. We all strive ... it's the pull of our innermost nature ... to experience more and more of what life has to offer us, and equally as important, what we have to offer life.

Dharma

I promise I will not get too philosophical. Actually this whole topic of full potential, higher states of consciousness, and enlightenment is what my next book is all about. *A Day in the Life of An Enlightened Person* is its title. I have written this down on my possibility/dream goal sheet. No, I don't have a date attached to it yet, since it's still just a possibility, a dream.

Enlightenment? Higher states of consciousness? What am I talking about? A person who is using their full potential. Full potential meaning:

- Unbounded energy
- Unlimited creative intelligence
- Infinite, immortal, eternal, bliss, love consciousness

Literally

Having the level of energy to have a clear, powerful mind throughout the day. Creative intelligence to know whatever you desire, whatever you put your attention on. The bliss of experience. Enjoying tidal waves of love and joy. 24 hours a day, 365 days of the year. Our birthright. Encoded in our DNA. A destiny for **all** of us.

Programmed within us is our dharma, a Sanskrit word meaning, "purpose." A purpose that makes full use of our unique individual talents. Think of the universe as a quadrillion jigsaw puzzle. As with any jigsaw puzzle each piece has its place. Each piece is important in filling out the full beauty of the puzzle. Puzzle is a good word here for two reasons, one it clearly illustrates the importance of each piece of the puzzle, and finding our dharma is a puzzle. It's something encoded into our being, but it is not something that is automatically handed to us. It is something that we must seek and find. If not now, when? as they say in the great Hebrew writings.

Part of the when, is the process, the unfolding. Yes, life is a journey, but it is also a destination. The destination of our full potential, the destination of living out our dharma, which is fulfilling for us, our family, our community, and our universe.

The stage we are at now can be compared to Beethoven sitting down at a piano with nine of his fingers bound together, and being asked to play the full glory of his symphonies. Our full potential would be being able to use all ten of our fingers.

Ancient books talk about powers that lie within us. One of the books by Patanjali lists 41 different powers that can be activated in higher states of consciousness. Activated is the key word here. We have these abilities, but we have not learned how to bring them out into the light of day.

Yes, we have the ability to heal ourselves from life threatening illnesses, but no, we haven't learned how to activate this ability. At least, not the great majority of us.

My Mission & My Dharma

My mission is to live permanently in the highest state of consciousness, the state of enlightenment. My dharma, my purpose in life, is to inspire people to better understand and experience higher states of consciousness and enlightenment.

I'm using goal setting and time management to enliven my mission and my dharma within my self. My vision is that I am a well known speaker on goal setting and time management, giving 108 seminars a year at full fee by 1996. I gave 87 workshops in 1995, not all at full fee. I will leverage this success to earn the right to then become a well known and respected speaker on higher states of consciousness and enlightenment. "Earn the right" meaning that I write that book while in a higher state of consciousness. Not theory, but a clear description of my own direct experience, and offering guidelines and guide posts for those seeking similar experiences.

A Heat Seeking Missile (& a Little Healthy Goal Bashing)

I have heard the mind described as a heat seeking missile. Supply it with a goal, and it will never veer off course until the goal is realized. I have also heard the mind described as a magical magnet. Powerful, specific, positive thoughts and goals attracting powerful and positive results. Napoleon Hill wrote extensively about this aspect of the mind in his classic, *Think and Grow Rich*.

All true, but not fully activated in most of us. It's influence is felt, but it's buried underneath that 90-99 percent of our potential that we are not using.

My goal is to live in this higher state of consciousness, and clearly describe its reality. To help people to move towards this reality for themselves.

But, as I promised, I won't get too philosophical. Just a glimpse into where I believe the goal setting process is taking me and you. I look forward to expanding upon this in my book on enlightenment.

The healthy goal bashing I'm referring to, is highlighted by two books I recently saw in a book store. *Stop Setting Goals* and *Living Without Goals*. The theme of each book is that goal setting can get you too narrow in your thinking, and that goal setting is not for everyone. That you can get too obsessive about your goals, close out other possibilities, and impede the creative, free flowing process.

I agree. We don't want you to become an anal retentive automaton who has no time for anything else but your specific, written goals. We need a healthy balance. I recommend that you write down your goals, look at them whenever the spirit moves you, to remind you of your commitments . . . then let it go.

Take action. Be spontaneous. Infuse a little innocence, and "Thy will be done," into the process. By doing this your goals will be achieved. I think it's healthy to bash goals so that we don't take all of this too seriously. Because seriousness, too much seriousness, can shut down the zone. Have fun. Focus your attention on what needs to be done, do it, and the results will unfold in their own good time. Write it down and let it go. Balance.

It's a Wrap—a Few Last Thoughts

"If you want something done give it to a busy person." Interesting. This ties in perfectly with the principle that work expands to fill the allotted time. This statement says a lot about managing multiple priorities, doing more with less, and about time management. I strongly believe that by doing just the two things that I recommend, 1) taking 15-30 minutes once a month to set down your upcoming months goals, and 2) taking 5-10 minutes to plan out your upcoming day, that these two alone will get you 80 percent of the way towards being a great time manager. Mix in a little "reality check" attitude, that life does get hectic and "wild and crazy" at times, and you'll be OK. Balancing desire with no whining. You'll still be busy, but busy with the activities that you choose to do. Those activities that will bring you personal and professional success.

CHAPTER TWELVE

With a Little Help from My Friends—Resources to Help You on Your Way

Recommended Audiocassettes

Listen to audiotapes. We already talked about the powerful and positive influence tapes can have on your life. Make it a habit. Here are some specific suggestions. These all can be ordered through Nightingale-Conant at 1-800-525-9000. Nightingale-Conant just celebrated their 35th year in business. Here are their top 20 best selling programs.

1. Lead the Field, Earl Nightingale
2. The Psychology of Winning, Dennis Waitley
3. How to Be A No-Limit Person, Wayne Dyer
4. Seeds of Greatness, Dennis Waitley
5. The Psychology of Achievement, Brian Tracy
6. The Psychology of Selling, Brian Tracy
7. The Secrets of Power Negotiating, Roger Dawson
8. The Psychology of High Self-Esteem, Nathaniel Branden
9. Winning Management Strategies for the Real World, Tom Peters
10. Unlimited Power, Anthony Robbins
11. Think and Grow Rich, Napoleon Hill
12. Thriving On Chaos, Tom Peters
13. Evelyn Wood Reading Dynamics, Evelyn Wood
14. Goals, Zig Ziglar

15. Personal Power, Anthony Robbins
16. The Awakened Life, Wayne Dyer
17. Mega Memory, Kevin Trudeau
18. Magical Mind, Magical Body, Deepak Chopra
19. The Silva Method, Robert Stone
20. Conversation Power, James Van Fleet

plus a few of my personal favorites (in no particular order) that didn't make this list:

— Power Negotiating for Salespeople, Roger Dawson
— Journey to the Boundless, Deepak Chopra
— The Art of Exceptional Living, Jim Rohn
— The 7 Habits of Highly Effective People, Stephen Covey

Recommended Books

Attend seminars, watch educational TV, and of course **read books**. Here are some of my favorites:

Personal Development
— *Think and Grow Rich*, Napoleon Hill
— *How to Win Friends and Influence People*, Dale Carnegie
— *The Power of Positive Thinking*, Norman Vincent Peale
— *Dress for Success*, John Malloy
— *Your Erroneous Zones*, Wayne Dyer
— *The Courage to Create*, Rollo May
— *Love Is Letting Go of Fear*, Gerald Jampolski
— *The Further Reaches of Human Nature*, Abraham Maslow
— *Man's Search for Meaning*, Victor Frankl
— *The Art of Loving*, Erich Fromm
— *Essays* by Ralph Waldo Emerson
— *The Magic of Thinking Big*, David Schwartz
— *The Richest Man in Babylon*, George Clason
— *Spiritual Economics*, Eric Butterworth
— *The Hundredth Monkey*, Ken Keyes, Jr.
— *The Hero with A Thousand Faces*, Joseph Campbell
— *Perfect Health*, Deepak Chopra
— *The Seven Spiritual Laws of Success*, Deepak Chopra
— *The Way of Life*, Lao Tzu

— *Siddhartha*, Herman Hesse
— *Demian*, Herman Hesse
— *The Science of Being, and the Art of Living*, Maharishi Mahesh Yogi
— *A Whack on the Side of the Head*, Roger von Oech
— Autobiography of Benjamin Franklin
— *Psycho-Cybernetics*, Maxwell Maltz
— *Stress Without Distress*, Hans Selye
— *The Road Less Traveled*, Scott Peck
— *Gilbert On Greatness*, Rob Gilbert
— *Everything I Need to Know I Learned in Kindergarten*, Robert Fulghum
— *Diamonds in the Rough*, Barry Farber
— *Dianetics: The Modern Science of Mental Health*, L. Ron Hubbard
— *Chicken Soup for the Soul*, Mark Victor Hanson and Jack Canfield
— *Tuesdays with Morrie*, Mitch Albom

Selling Skills
— *The Greatest Salesman in the World*, Og Mandino
— *See you At the Top*, Zig Ziglar
— *How to Master the Art of Selling*, Tom Hopkins
— *Back to Basic Selling*, Bob Taylor
— *Selling Through Negotiation*, Homer Smith
— *The Discipline of Selling*, Jim Evered
— *The Lacy Techniques of Salesmanship*
— *How to Sell Anything to Anybody*, Joe Girard
— *Supersellers*, Gerhard Gschwandtner
— *The Perfect Sales Presentation*, Robert Shook
— *Relationship Selling*, Jim Cathcart
— *How to Develop A Six Figure Income in Real Estate*, Mike Ferry
— *How to List and Sell Real Estate*, Danielle Kennedy
— *The One Minute Salesperson*, Larry Wilson
— *Strategic Selling*, Miller & Heiman
— *Spin Selling*, Neil Rackham
— *What It Takes to Succeed in Sales*, Jeanne and Herb Greenberg
— *Motivating with Sales Contests*, David Worman
— *Prospecting your Way to Sales Success*, Bill Good
— *Getting to Yes*, Fisher & Ury
— *Swim with the Sharks*, Harvey Mackay

- *Marketing Warfare*, Trout & Ries
- *How I Raised Myself from Failure to Success in Selling*, Frank Bettger
- *Consultative Selling*, Mack Hanan
- *The Psychology of Overcoming Call Reluctance*, Dudley & Goodman
- *How to Sell Against Competition and Win*, Bill Subers
- *Cold Calling Techniques That Really Work*, Stephen Schiffman
- *Niche Selling*, William Brooks
- *Dynamic Professional Selling*, Arnold Schwartz
- *How to Make Big Money Selling*, Joe Gandolfo
- *Changing the Game, Selling in the 90's*, Larry Wilson
- *From Selling to Managing*, Ronald Brown
- *Breakthrough Selling*, Barry Farber

Management Development
- *The One Minute Manager*, Ken Blanchard
- *The Effective Executive*, Peter Drucker
- *The Power of Wow*, Tom Peters
- *Moments of Truth*, Jan Carlson
- *Flawless Consulting*, Peter Block
- *What Color is Your Parachute?*, Richard Bolles
- *The Marketing Imagination*, Theodore Levitt
- *The Time Trap*, Alec Mackenzie
- *If You Don't Have the Time to Do It Right, When Will You Find the Time to Do It Over?*, Jeffrey Mayer
- *How to Get Control of your Time and Your Life*, Alan Lakein
- *Leadership Effectiveness Training*, Tom Gordon
- *The Leadership Challenge*, Kouzes & Posner
- *How to Get Your Point Across in 30 Seconds or Less*, Milo Frank
- *Megatrends 2000*, Naisbitt & Aburdene
- *The 7 Habits of Highly Effective People*, Stephen Covey
- *Situational Leadership*, Hershy & Blanchard
- *Coaching for Improved Work Performance*, Ferdinand Fournies
- *The Consultants Calling*, Jeffrey Bellman
- *Mastery*, George Leonard
- *The Strategic Coach*, Dan Sullivan
- *The E-Myth Revisited*, Michael Gerber

Motivational Quotes

Reminders to inspire us to take action. I know where a few originally came from, all the others I've seen and heard over the years.

The key to success is constancy of purpose.

Reasons are the fuel in the furnace of achievement. It's the power of why.

"When I took over the Dolphins in 1970, the press wanted to know what my three- or five-year plan was. I told them my plan was day-to-day."
Don Shula, Miami Dolphins Coach

"Choose work you love, and you will never have to work a day in your life."
Confucius

Learn to be comfortable with being uncomfortable.

"Doing my best is not the best I can do."
Zach Sapolsky, High School Student

"Do not make me the beneficiary of your poor planning."
Steven J. Levitt, Financial Director

The important thing is not what happens when you're setting the goals, but what happens when you're following-through out there all alone making it happen.

"Common sense is not common practice."
"The main thing is to keep the main thing the main thing."
"First things first and last things never."
Stephen Covey

"The bottom line in life is that if you're not doing something it's because you associate more pain in doing it than not doing it."
Tony Robbins

Action, the antidote for fear, is also the best teacher. There is truth in the old saying:
> I hear; I forget.
> I see; I remember.
> I do; I understand.

It is not your commitment that you should be worried about, it is your commitment to your commitment.

Successful people hate to do the same things that unsuccessful people hate to do, but they discipline themselves to do it anyway.

"I never hurry and never work quickly, but I do twice as much work as any one else, because I always do exactly what needs to be done."
Anonymous

10 Tips to Stop Whining & Start Winning
1. Know when you're whining and decide to stop
2. Create a mission
3. Set goals
4. Write down your goals
5. Become unstoppable
6. Take action/take risks
7. Believe in what you're doing
8. Have a "can do" attitude
9. Be focused
10. Conquer fatigue

—from my audiotape of the same name

When we get overwhelmed there is a tendency to start whining, so remember:
> Inch by inch is a cinch;
> Yard by yard is hard.

"We must start thinking big . . . create a supreme goal, and that will come true. Think big and you will accomplish it. Don't desire for anything less than the best. Don't desire for anything less than the highest. You will get what you desire."
Maharishi Mahesh Yogi

"Follow your bliss."
Joseph Campbell

What I seek is seeking me.
        This is true for all of us.

"Whoever saves one life, saves the entire world."
Talmud

"I have to do it myself, and I can't do it alone."
Pecos River Learning Centers

"Go as far as you can, with all that you've got."
Larry Wilson

"Go as far as you can see, and when you get there, you'll see more."
Dick Manning

"God, grant me the serenity to accept the things I cannot change,
The courage to change the things I can,
And the wisdom to know the difference."
known as The Serenity Prayer

"Be the change you are creating."
Mahatma Ghandi

"The greatest discovery of my time is that human beings can alter their lives by altering their attitudes."
William James

"So, let it be written. So, let it be done."
Yul Brynner in "The Ten Commandments"
and "The King and I"

"Do the thing you fear and the death of fear is certain."
"Nothing great was ever accomplished without enthusiasm."
Ralph Waldo Emerson

"Those who cannot remember the past are condemned to repeat it."
George Santayana

"The history of man is the history of people selling themselves short."
Abraham Maslow

"Most people's jobs are too small for their spirits."
Anonymous

"The plan is nothing, planning is everything."
"Never complain, never explain."
Benjamin Disraeli

"For of all sad words of tongue or pen, the saddest are these, "it might have been."
John Greenleaf Whittier

"Options are the key to mental health. The goal achievement process creates powerful options for anyone and everyone."
Laurane Magliari

"The basic cause of illness is unhappiness, and the great healer is joy."
Rabbi Nachman of Breslov

"Character strength comes from a long process of dealing with adversity."
Thomas A. Edison

"What are the two most important days in your life? Today and tomorrow."

Joseph Weissman

The Basic Issues of Life
What?

What is my purpose in this world?
What am I doing with my life?
What are my true goals?
To what extent am I achieving them, and if I am not, why not?
And how, with help, can I overcome these barriers in order to attain complete self fulfillment?

Anonymous

"What is the best use of my time right now?"

Brian Tracy

"It's not about ability, it's about heart."

Gay Kobat

"Life is good and the best is yet to come."
"Balance is having your head in the clouds and your feet on the ground."

Mark Riesenberg

"Life is filled with obstacle illusions."

Michael Wells

"Time management is not about doing more things faster, even though this may happen. It's about doing the right things right."
"Managers do things right. Leaders do the right things."
"In the absence of clearly defined goals we tend to focus on activity and ultimately become consumed by it."

Peter Drucker

"Luck is the residue of design."

Branch Rickey

"The true measure of success in life isn't money, fame or power. It's laugh lines."

Anonymous

"It's not the dream but the dreamer who can make it all come true. Keep that in mind and remember it's always up to you. Quitters never win and winners never quit."

Eddie Williams

A Powerful Short Story

A while back I was reading about an expert on the subject of time management. One day this expert was speaking to a group of business students, and to drive home a point, uses an illustration those students will never forget.

As this man stood in front of the group he said, "Okay, time for a quiz." Then he pulled out a one gallon, wide mouthed mason jar and set it on a table in front of him. Then he produced about a dozen fist-sized rocks and carefully placed them, one at a time, into the jar. When the jar was filled to the top and no more rocks would fit inside, he asked, "Is this jar full?" Everyone in the class said, "Yes."

When he said, "Really?" He reached under the table and pulled out a bucket of gravel. Then he dumped some gravel in and shook the jar causing pieces of gravel to work themselves into the spaces between the rocks. Then he asked the group once more, "Is the jar full?" By this time the class was onto him. "Probably not," one of them answered.

"Good!" he replied. He reached under the table and brought out a bucket full of sand. He started dumping the sand in and it went into all the spaces left between the rocks and the gravel. Once more he asked the question, "Is this jar full?" "No!" the class shouted.

Once again he said, "Good!" Then he grapped a pitcher of water and began to pour it in until the jar was filled to the brim. Then he looked up at the class and asked, "What is the point of this illustration?"

One eager beaver raised his hand and said, "The point is, no matter how full your schedule is, if you try really hard, you can always fit some more things into it." "No," the teacher replied, "that's not the point. The truth this illustration teaches us is: If you don't put the big rocks in first, you'll never get them in at all."

What are the big rocks in your life? A project that YOU want to accomplish? Time with your loved ones? Your faith, your education, your finances? A cause? Teaching or mentoring others? Business goals that really motivate you?

Remember to put these BIG ROCKS in first or you'll never get them in at all.

So, tonight or in the morning when you are reflecting on this short story, ask yourself this question, What are the 'big rocks' in my life or business? Then, put those in your jar first.

Excerpts from two of my favorite poems:

"...that serene and blessed mood,
In which the affections gently lead us on,-
Until, the breath of this corporeal frame
And even the motion of our human blood
Almost suspended, we are laid asleep
In body; and become a living soul:
While with an eye made quiet by the power
Of harmony, and the deep power of joy,
We see into the life of things."

Tintern Abbey,
William Wordsworth

"There was a time when meadow, grove, and stream,
The earth, and every common sight,
    To me did seem
      Apparelled in celestial light,
The glory and the freshness of a dream."

"It is not now as it hath been of yore;-
    Turn whereso'er I may,
      By night or day,
The things which I have seen I now can see no more."

Intimations of Immortality
William Wordsworth

To see a world
In a grain of sand

And a heaven
In a wild flower

Hold infinity
In the palm of your hand

And eternity
In an hour.

William Blake

My Monthly Goals

For the month of _____

Whining 🚫

Personal Goals
_____
_____

Family Goals
_____
_____

Business Goals
_____
_____
_____
_____
_____
_____
_____
_____
_____
_____
_____
_____

© 1999 Human Resources Unlimited

Monthly Form

My Monthly Goals
For the month of _____ No Whining

Personal Goals

Family Goals

Business Goals

© 1999 Human Resources Unlimited

My Monthly Goals
For the month of _____ No Whining

Personal Goals

Family Goals

Business Goals

© 1999 Human Resources Unlimited

My Monthly Goals
For the month of _____ No Whining

Personal Goals

Family Goals

Business Goals

© 1999 Human Resources Unlimited

My Monthly Goals
For the month of _____ No Whining

Personal Goals

Family Goals

Business Goals

© 1999 Human Resources Unlimited

Four-Part Monthly Form

My Goals

Personal Goals
_____
_____

Family Goals
_____
_____
_____

Business Goals
_____
_____
_____
_____
_____
_____
_____
_____
_____
_____
_____
_____
_____

© 1999 Human Resources Unlimited

Long Term Goals

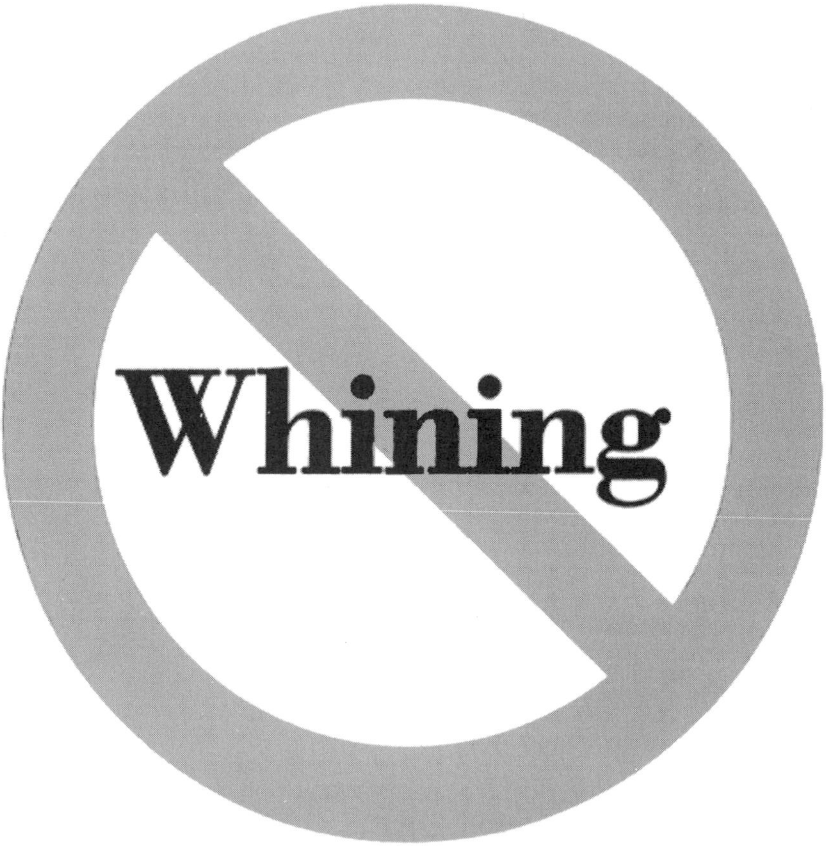

Stop Whining and Start Winning

29 Gilbert Place
West Orange, NJ 07052
(973) 736-8112 Phone
(973) 736-9522 Fax
E-Mail: hrunltd@aol.com
Website: www.hrugoals.com

Mark Riesenberg • President

Give the Gift of Goals to Your Friends, Family and Colleagues

$19.95
volume discounts available

Check your local Bookstore, Amazon.com, or contact

Mark Riesenberg
Human Resources Unlimited
29 Gilbert Place
West Orange, NJ 07052
1-800-269-4463 Phone
(973) 736-9522 Fax

☐ YES, I am interested in having Mark Riesenberg speak or give a seminar to my company, association, school, or organization. Please send information to:

NAME _____

PHONE _____

ORGANIZATION _____

ADDRESS _____

CITY/STATE/ZIP _____